EatRight
Heart Smart

EatRight
Heart Smart

Oxmoor
House®

EatRight Heart Smart from the EatRight series
Copyright 1997 by Oxmoor House, Inc.
Book Division of Southern Progress Corporation
P.O. Box 2463, Birmingham, Alabama 35201

Library of Congress Catalog Number: 97-69954
ISBN: 0-8487-1599-3

Manufactured in the United States of America
First Printing 1997

Be sure to check with your health-care provider before making any changes in your diet.

Editor-in-Chief: Nancy Fitzpatrick Wyatt
Senior Foods Editor: Katherine M. Eakin
Senior Editor, Editorial Services: Olivia Kindig Wells
Art Director: James Boone

EatRight Heart Smart

Oxmoor House
Editor: Anne Chappell Cain, M.S., M.P.H., R.D.
Designer: Barbara Ball
Copy Editor: Shari K. Wimberly
Editorial Assistant: Allison D. Ingram
Intern: Andrea Noble
Director, Test Kitchens: Kathleen Royal Phillips
Assistant Director, Test Kitchens: Gayle Hays Sadler
Photography Test Kitchens Staff: Susan Hall Bellows, Julie Christopher,
    Michele Brown Fuller, Natalie E. King, Elizabeth Tyler Luckett, Jan Moon,
    Iris Crawley O'Brien, Jan A. Smith
Senior Photographer: Jim Bathie
Senior Photo Stylist: Kay E. Clarke
Production Director: Phillip Lee
Associate Production Manager: Vanessa Cobbs Richardson
Production Assistant: Faye Porter Bonner

The University of Alabama at Birmingham
Senior Author: Roland L. Weinsier, M.D., Dr.P.H., Professor and Chairman,
    Department of Nutrition Sciences, School of Health Related Professions,
    School of Medicine, School of Dentistry
Co-Authors: Nedra P. Wilson, M.S., R.D., Associate Professor,
    Sarah L. Morgan, M.D., FACP, FADA, M.S., R.D., Associate Professor,
    Beth F. Bussey, M.S., R.D.,
    Annie R. Cornwell, M.S., R.D., Associate Professor
Contributors: Rebecca L. Bradley, M.A., R.D., Associate Professor,
    Carol B. Craig, M.S., R.D., Professor
Writer: Virginia Gilbert Loftin
Recipe Home Economist: Jan Terry Tennant
Recipe Typist: Kathy Franklin

Page 2: *Mexican Salad (page 61)*

We're Here for You!
We at Oxmoor House are dedicated to serving you with reliable information that expands your imagination and enriches your life. We welcome your comments and suggestions. Please write to us at:

Oxmoor House, Inc.
Editor, *EatRight Heart Smart*
2100 Lakeshore Drive
Birmingham, AL 35209

To order additional publications, call 1-205-877-6560.

CONTENTS

PREFACE   6

EATRIGHT FOR A HEALTHY HEART   7

WHAT'S YOUR RISK OF HEART ATTACK?   8

3 SMART STEPS FOR A HEALTHY HEART   11

THE EATRIGHT PROGRAM   18

EATRIGHT RECIPES

APPETIZERS   27

BREADS   31

FISH AND SHELLFISH   41

GRAINS, PASTAS, AND LEGUMES   49

MEATLESS MAIN DISHES   59

MEATS   71

POULTRY   83

SALADS   99

SOUPS   107

VEGETABLES   115

SPECIAL OCCASION   125

RECIPE INDEX   138

SUBJECT INDEX   144

PREFACE

The EatRight program was developed in 1976 by a team of physicians, dietitians, and psychologists at The University of Alabama at Birmingham and is one of the longest running and most successful weight-control programs in the country.

But EatRight is more than a diet. It's a safe, nutritionally sound, and heart-smart eating plan that helps put you in control of your health.

If you need to lose weight, the plan provides the information and motivational tips to get you to your desired weight. And to maintain your weight and improve your eating habits, you'll find the EatRight method simple to follow and easy to remember.

EatRight cuts fat, cholesterol, and sodium, while it adds fiber and important nutrients that are known to reduce your risk of heart disease. Best of all, EatRight is built on a variety of great-tasting foods that won't leave you feeling hungry.

Welcome to the EatRight program, and to a heart-smart way of living—for life.

Roland L. Weinsier, M.D., Dr.P.H.
Professor and Chairman,
*   Department of Nutrition Sciences*
Schools of Health Related Professions,
*   Medicine, and Dentistry*
The University of Alabama at
*   Birmingham*

EatRight for a Healthy Heart

THE HEART-SMART STEPS FOR HEALTHY EATING

1. EAT MORE VEGETABLES AND FRUITS.

2. EAT LESS FAT, CHOLESTEROL, AND SODIUM.

3. EAT MORE HEART-SMART NUTRIENTS THAT REDUCE YOUR RISK OF HEART DISEASE.

Cardiovascular disease accounts for about 1 million deaths in the United States each year. And many more Americans are at risk for developing heart disease because they eat too much fat and don't exercise enough. Extensive medical research over the past several decades has given us the following facts about heart disease:

◆ Smoking and stress are bad for your heart.

◆ Physical activity is good for your heart.

◆ Being overweight puts you at greater risk for cardiovascular disease than those who maintain their recommended weights.

◆ High levels of blood cholesterol can narrow, harden, and clog arteries, raising the risk of stroke and heart attack.

But lifestyle changes such as losing weight, kicking the smoking habit, reducing stress, and getting at least 30 minutes of physical activity three or four days a week can lower the risk of heart disease.

While there is still much more to learn about the causes of heart disease and how to treat it, one verdict is in. Diet plays a critical role in heart health, and the EatRight program can help you take the steps that lead to heart-smart eating.

WHAT'S YOUR RISK OF HEART ATTACK?

The next three pages will help you determine your risk of heart attack. Review the risk factor information, and complete the Heart Risk Quiz on page 10.

BLOOD PRESSURE POINTERS

Blood pressure is measured with two numbers: **systolic** and **diastolic**. The **systolic** (top) number is pressure in the blood vessels during a heart contraction. The **diastolic** (bottom) number represents the level of pressure between contractions. If either number is too high, that means that the heart is working harder than normal to pump blood through the body, and that the vessels are under excessive pressure. See the chart below for optimal blood pressure numbers.

Blood Pressure (mm/Hg)	Optimal	Normal	High Normal	High Blood Pressure
Systolic (top number)	less than 120	less than 130	130–139	140 or higher
Diastolic (bottom number)	less than 80	less than 85	85–89	90 or higher

PHYSICAL ACTIVITY

Regular physical activity helps reduce your risk of heart disease. Choose the column (A, B, or C) that best describes your usual level of physical activity.

A Highly Active

My job requires very hard physical labor (such as digging or loading heavy objects) at least four hours a day.

OR I do vigorous activities (jogging, cycling, swimming) at least three times per week for 30 to 60 minutes or more.

OR I do at least one hour of moderate activity such as brisk walking at least four days a week.

B Moderately Active

My job requires that I walk, lift, carry, or do other moderately hard work for several hours per day (day care worker, stock clerk, waitress, or waiter).

OR I spend much of my leisure time doing moderate activities (dancing, gardening, walking, or housework).

C Inactive

My job requires that I sit at a desk most of the day.

AND Much of my leisure time is spent in sedentary activities (watching TV, reading).

AND I seldom work up a sweat, and I cannot walk fast without having to stop to catch my breath.

BODY MASS INDEX

Body Mass Index (BMI) is a height-weight calculation that you can use to determine if your weight is in a healthy range. BMI is a more accurate measurement of your body fat than the former "ideal" weights listed in life insurance weight tables.

To use the BMI table below:
1. Find your height in inches on the left side of the table.
2. On the row corresponding to your height, find your current weight.
3. Then look at the numbers at the very top of the column to find your BMI.
4. Use the table below to determine your health risk.

BMI	19	21	23	25	27	30	32	34	36	38	40
HEIGHT					WEIGHT (POUNDS)						
58"	91	100	110	119	129	143	152	162	172	181	191
59"	94	104	114	124	134	149	159	169	179	188	198
60"	97	107	117	127	138	153	163	173	183	194	204
61"	101	111	122	132	143	159	169	180	191	201	212
62"	103	114	125	136	147	163	174	185	196	206	217
63"	107	119	130	141	152	169	181	192	203	214	226
64"	111	123	135	146	158	176	187	199	211	223	234
65"	114	126	138	150	162	180	192	204	216	228	240
66"	118	131	143	156	168	187	199	212	224	236	249
67"	121	134	147	159	172	191	204	217	229	242	255
68"	125	139	152	165	178	198	211	224	238	251	264
69"	128	142	155	169	182	203	216	230	243	257	270
70"	133	147	161	175	189	210	224	237	251	265	279
71"	136	150	164	179	193	214	229	243	257	271	286
72"	140	155	170	185	199	221	236	251	266	281	295
73"	143	158	174	189	204	226	241	257	272	287	302
74"	148	164	179	195	210	234	249	265	281	296	312

BMI AND HEALTH RISK

19–24	Healthy Weight
25–26	Low Risk
27–29	Moderate Risk
30–34	High Risk
35+	Very High Risk

For example, if you are 5 feet 7 inches (67") and weigh 159 pounds, your BMI is 25. This means you have a low risk of developing a weight-related disease like heart disease or Type 2 diabetes.

Adapted from: Weighing the Options: Criteria for Evaluating Weight-Management Programs. Washington, D.C.: National Academy of Sciences, 1995.

Heart Risk Quiz

Are you at risk for a heart attack? Take this quiz to find out. If your score is high, you can lower your risk by following the steps on pages 11–17.

Instructions: In each risk category below, circle the number next to the statement that's most true for you.

Cigarette Smoking

I never smoked or stopped smoking three or more years ago.	1
I don't smoke but live and/or work with smokers.	2
I stopped smoking within the last three years.	3
I smoke regularly.	4
I smoke regularly and live and/or work with smokers.	5

Total Blood Cholesterol

Use the number from your most recent blood cholesterol measurement.

Less than 160	1
160–199	2
Don't know	3
200–239	4
240 or higher	5

HDL ("Good") Cholesterol

Use the number from your most recent HDL cholesterol measurement.

Over 60	1
50–60	2
Don't know	3
35–55	4
Less than 35	5

Systolic Blood Pressure

Use the first (top) number from your most recent blood pressure measurement.

Less than 120	1
120–139	2
Don't know	3
140–159	4
160 or higher	5

Excess Body Weight

See the Body Mass Index (BMI) table on page 9.

I have a BMI of less than 25.	1
I have a BMI of 25–26.	2
I have a BMI of 27–29.	3
I have a BMI of 30–34.	4
I have a BMI of greater than 35.	5

Rating Your Activity Level

Circle the number corresponding to the statement that most closely describes your activity level (see Physical Activity, page 8).

Your physical activity is more like A	1
Between A and B	2
Your physical activity is more like B	3
Between B and C	4
Your physical activity is more like C	5

Total _____

Scoring

Add the numbers corresponding to your answers to determine your total score.

If your total score is:	Your heart attack risk is:
6–13	Low
14–22	Moderate
23–30	High

Your score is simply an estimate of your possible risk. A high score doesn't mean you'll definitely have a heart attack; a low score doesn't mean you're safe from heart disease. Check your individual category scores to see which factors are increasing your risk the most.

3 SMART STEPS FOR A HEALTHY HEART

Research over the past 30 years has clearly shown that diet and heart disease are related, and three simple steps can start you on your way to a healthy heart.

The three steps are medically proven, easy to remember, and can be accomplished today, starting right now: Eat more vegetables and fruits; eat less fat, cholesterol, and sodium; eat more heart-smart nutrients that reduce your risk of heart disease.

Each step naturally leads to the others. If you just start eating more vegetables and fruits (which are low in fat, cholesterol, and sodium), you'll be eating less fat. And vegetables and fruits are primary sources of the nutrients known to specifically play a role in heart disease prevention.

1. Eat more vegetables and fruits.

When your mother told you to eat your vegetables, she may not have been thinking about preventing a heart attack. But her advice was right on the mark.

Vegetables and fruits are the mainstay of the heart-healthy EatRight plan. Fresh fruits and vegetables are naturally low in fat and calories, and high in fiber. Equally important, they contain complex carbohydrates, which are easily converted into the body's main source of energy.

Those high in water-soluble fiber can even *reduce cholesterol* when incorporated into a diet low in saturated fat. You'll reap this extra benefit when you eat soluble fiber-containing fruits and vegetables like apricots, figs, prunes, Brussels sprouts, and a variety of dried beans and peas.

And consider this: By getting more of your calories from vegetables and fruits than from meats, sweets, and fatty foods, you'll increase your intake of heart-smart nutrients including vitamins C and E, calcium, magnesium, potassium, and fiber.

There is yet another advantage to eating vegetables and fruits. Because they tend to take longer to eat and leave you feeling more satisfied than high-fat, low-fiber foods, you'll be less tempted to snack on foods that aren't as good for you.

TOP 10 VEGGIES AND FRUITS

Because they contain high amounts of heart-healthy nutrients, these vegetables are some of your smartest choices:

1. Asparagus
2. Broccoli
3. Brussels sprouts
4. Cabbage
5. Cantaloupe
6. Kale
7. Oranges
8. Spinach
9. Strawberries
10. Sweet Potatoes

---

2. Eat less fat, cholesterol, and sodium.

To reduce your chances of developing heart disease, eat less fat, cholesterol, and sodium. Fat and cholesterol clog your blood vessels; sodium can raise blood pressure, increasing the risk of heart attack and stroke.

The EatRight plan uses fat sparingly, limiting it to a maximum number of servings each day according to your calorie level. You don't have to count fat grams, but if you do, you'll see that only about 20 to 25 percent of total EatRight calories come from fat (that's *below* the American Heart Association's recommendation of no more than 30 percent of total calories from fat).

Bad Fat, Better Fat?

The type of fat you eat can be as important to your heart's health as the amount of fat in your diet. Fats contain **saturated, polyunsaturated,** and **monounsaturated** fatty acids. Most fats are a mixture of these three but are classified by the one that predominates.

Saturated fats are mostly in foods of animal origin: butter, lard, meat, and poultry skin. But you'll also find them in palm kernel oil and coconut oil. Saturated fats are firm at room temperature. These are the fats that raise the level of harmful cholesterol in your blood the most; they should make up no more than one-third of your total fat intake.

Polyunsaturated fats are primarily found in plants, not in animal products, and are liquid at room temperature. Sources include nuts, sunflower seeds, and vegetable oils such as corn, safflower, and sunflower. These fats can lower blood levels of total cholesterol. Less than one-third of your total fat should come from polyunsaturated fats.

Monounsaturated fats also come from plant foods, and are found in avocados, nuts, and peanut, canola, and olive oils. These fats can help lower total cholesterol and can also increase the ratio of good cholesterol to bad cholesterol (See "What Is Cholesterol?" on page 13). One-third to one-half of your total fat calories should come from monounsaturated fats.

Generally, the softer and more pourable the fat, the less harmful it is to your heart. The exceptions are palm, coconut, and palm kernel oils, which are high in saturated fat. By choosing fats wisely and using them sparingly, you can eat well *and* enjoy the benefits of a heart-healthy diet.

AMERICAN HEART ASSOCIATION DIETARY RECOMMENDATIONS

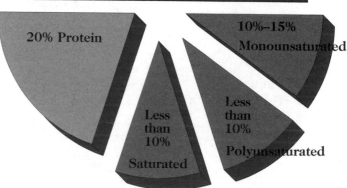
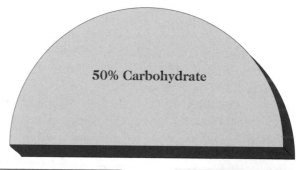

50% Carbohydrate

20% Protein

10%–15% Monounsaturated

Less than 10% Saturated

Less than 10% Polyunsaturated

30% Total Fat

TRANS FAT

There's another kind of fat lurking in your food, and it's a bad one. **Trans fatty acids** are created when food is "partially hydrogenated," meaning hydrogen has been added for firmness and stability. Vegetable shortening is an example of a fat that has been partially hydrogenated. Trans fatty acids raise cholesterol about as much as saturated fats do, so a heart-healthy diet should contain only tiny amounts of trans fat.

Trans fatty acids have not yet been included in labeling regulations by the Food and Drug Administration (FDA). Foods labeled "no cholesterol," "low cholesterol," or "made with vegetable oil" may actually contain high amounts of artery-clogging trans fat. Fast-food items cooked in partially hydrogenated shortening are likely loaded with trans fat.

Ways To Avoid Trans Fat

◆ Use tub, squeeze, and spray versions of fat-free or reduced-fat margarine.
◆ Use olive oil instead of partially hydrogenated vegetable oils.
◆ Don't eat fried foods.
◆ Limit intake of foods than contain vegetable shortening or partially hydrogenated oil.

WHAT IS CHOLESTEROL?

Cholesterol is the white, waxy fat your body produces to build cell walls and make certain hormones. Dietary cholesterol is found only in animal products. You add to your natural supply when you eat high-cholesterol foods. Excess cholesterol in the blood is a risk factor for heart disease because it builds up along blood vessel walls and constricts blood flow.

Good vs. Bad. Cholesterol travels through the blood in packages called **lipoproteins**. Low-density lipoproteins (LDL) carry cholesterol to the walls of the blood vessels, while high-density lipoproteins (HDL) take cholesterol to the liver where it is used or eliminated. So LDL is known as "bad" cholesterol, and HDL is called "good" cholesterol.

Do the Numbers. Have your cholesterol level checked periodically as part of your routine medical care, and more often if you have been diagnosed with heart disease. Your HDL and LDL values are just as important as your total cholesterol when determining your risk for heart disease (see chart below).

Cholesterol Countdown. Heredity and gender affect cholesterol levels. Until menopause, women tend to have lower levels of total cholesterol; after menopause, their average level surpasses that of men. You can't change genetic and gender factors, but you can change your diet and increase your physical activity to lower cholesterol enough to reduce your risk of heart disease.

If you lower your total cholesterol by 15 percent, you could drop your risk of heart disease by almost a third.

Cholesterol Levels (mg/dl)	Desirable	Borderline-High	High-Risk
Total cholesterol	less than 200	200–239	240 or higher
LDL	less than 130	130–159	160 or higher
HDL	35 or higher	less than 35	less than 35

What about Sodium?

Limiting salt and other sodium is another important key to a healthy heart. Salt accounts for most of the sodium in your diet, but sodium also is found in many natural and processed foods and in medications. Although the body needs it in tiny amounts, excess sodium can raise blood pressure, increasing your risk of heart attack, stroke, and kidney disease.

The American Heart Association's recommendation for sodium is no more than 2,400 milligrams per day.

Halt the Salt

Use the following tips to help you shake the salt habit:

◆ Cut back on salt intake gradually, giving your tastebuds time to adjust.

◆ Don't add salt to your food during cooking. Instead, use herbs and spices for extra zest.

◆ Avoid high-sodium flavor enhancers like garlic salt, celery salt, onion salt, or MSG.

◆ Read the labels on packaged and processed foods because high-sodium foods don't always taste salty. Avoid products with more than 15 percent daily value for sodium.

◆ Limit your intake of cheese, luncheon meats, and other processed meats.

◆ Limit your intake of condiments like soy sauce, ketchup, mustard, salad dressings, pickles, and olives.

◆ Choose low-salt crackers, chips, and snacks.

◆ Choose no-salt-added or low-sodium versions of canned vegetables and soups.

How to Read a Food Label

If you're trying to eat for a healthy heart, start reading food labels and checking the calories, fat, cholesterol, and sodium.

New FDA labeling standards take effect by the end of 1997. The following definitions should make it easier for you to make healthy choices at the supermarket, especially in the dairy and meat sections.

Dairy Products

Reduced-fat: Products that have 5 grams of fat or less per serving. That includes 2% milk, which has about 4.5 grams of fat per 1-cup serving.
Low-fat and light: Products with 3 grams of fat or less per serving, such as 1% milk.
Skim, nonfat, and fat-free: Products with less than 0.5 gram of fat per serving.

The new labeling rules also apply to cottage cheese and sour cream. Most yogurt products already follow the standards voluntarily. However, the rules do not apply to "light" whipping cream, which is called "light" to distinguish it from heavy cream.

Meat, Poultry, and Fish

Lean: Meat, poultry, or fish that contains less than 10 grams of fat, less than 4 grams of saturated fat, and less than 95 milligrams of cholesterol per 3-ounce serving.
Extra lean: Contains less than 5 grams of fat, less than 2 grams of saturated fat, and less than 95 milligrams of cholesterol per 3-ounce serving.
Fresh: The new label standards will restrict the term to poultry that has never been refrigerated colder than 26°F.
Natural: Meat or poultry that contains no artificial ingredients or added color, and that has been processed only minimally. (This term does not mean that natural ingredients like water and salt have not been added during processing, or that the animal has not been given antibiotics or hormones.)

SAMPLE LABEL

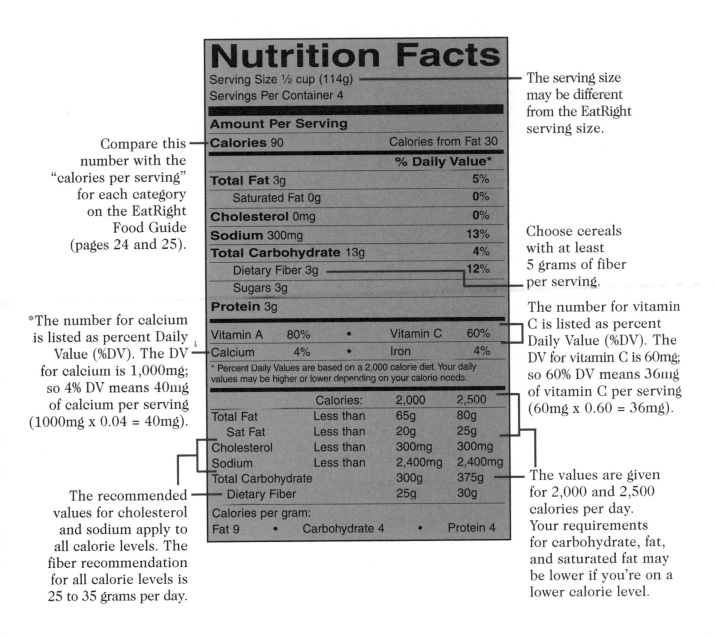

Compare this number with the "calories per serving" for each category on the EatRight Food Guide (pages 24 and 25).

The serving size may be different from the EatRight serving size.

Choose cereals with at least 5 grams of fiber per serving.

*The number for calcium is listed as percent Daily Value (%DV). The DV for calcium is 1,000mg; so 4% DV means 40mg of calcium per serving (1000mg x 0.04 = 40mg).

The number for vitamin C is listed as percent Daily Value (%DV). The DV for vitamin C is 60mg; so 60% DV means 36mg of vitamin C per serving (60mg x 0.60 = 36mg).

The recommended values for cholesterol and sodium apply to all calorie levels. The fiber recommendation for all calorie levels is 25 to 35 grams per day.

The values are given for 2,000 and 2,500 calories per day. Your requirements for carbohydrate, fat, and saturated fat may be lower if you're on a lower calorie level.

Nutrition Facts

Serving Size ½ cup (114g)
Servings Per Container 4

Amount Per Serving

Calories 90	Calories from Fat 30

	% Daily Value*
Total Fat 3g	5%
Saturated Fat 0g	0%
Cholesterol 0mg	0%
Sodium 300mg	13%
Total Carbohydrate 13g	4%
Dietary Fiber 3g	12%
Sugars 3g	
Protein 3g	

Vitamin A	80%	•	Vitamin C	60%
Calcium	4%	•	Iron	4%

* Percent Daily Values are based on a 2,000 calorie diet. Your daily values may be higher or lower depending on your calorie needs.

	Calories:	2,000	2,500
Total Fat	Less than	65g	80g
Sat Fat	Less than	20g	25g
Cholesterol	Less than	300mg	300mg
Sodium	Less than	2,400mg	2,400mg
Total Carbohydrate		300g	375g
Dietary Fiber		25g	30g

Calories per gram:
Fat 9 • Carbohydrate 4 • Protein 4

*Although the adult Recommended Daily Allowance (RDA) for calcium is 800 milligrams, the Daily Value is 1,000 milligrams because it's based on an average of the recommended amounts for teenagers, pregnant and breastfeeding women, and adults over age 19 years.

3. Eat more heart-smart nutrients that reduce your risk of heart disease.

Based on current knowledge, it's clear that certain vitamins and minerals may lower your risk of heart disease.

Vitamins are organic chemical compounds that regulate all body processes. **Minerals** are inorganic substances that help give your body structure and, along with vitamins, regulate body processes.

The vitamins and minerals that play a role in the prevention of heart disease are vitamins **C and E, folate, calcium, magnesium,** and **potassium**. There is also another group of compounds, called **phytochemicals,** that appears to help reduce the risk of heart disease.

Use the chart below as a guide to heart-healthy nutrients, Recommended Daily Allowances (RDAs) for adults, good food sources, and a few recipes in this cookbook that contain significant levels of each of the nutrients.

VITAMIN C

Heart-Smart Function
Vitamin C is an antioxidant. It blocks oxidation, the chemical process by which LDL ("bad" cholesterol) builds up and hardens along arterial walls.
RDA: 60 milligrams

Food Sources
Broccoli, Brussels sprouts, cabbage, cauliflower, citrus fruits and juices, greens, mangoes, melons, papaya, peppers (all varieties), strawberries

Recipe/Page Number
Sweet-and-Sour Swordfish, 46
Hearty Barley, 65
Stuffed Green Peppers, 72
Blueberry-Melon Salad, 100
Fresh Fruit with Ginger-
    Yogurt Dressing, 101
Zesty Cauliflower Salad, 104
Cheesy Potato-Broccoli
    Soup, 108
Orange Crêpes, 130

VITAMIN E

Heart-Smart Function
Vitamin E functions as an antioxidant and blocks oxidation, the chemical process by which LDL ("bad" cholesterol) builds up and hardens along arterial walls.
RDA: 10 milligrams

Food Sources
Almonds, blackberries, canola oil, fortified cereals, green leafy vegetables, margarine*, mayonnaise*, salad dressings*, sunflower seeds, sweet potatoes, walnuts, whole grains

*Regular, not fat-free

Recipe/Page Number
Cauliflower Nuggets, 29
Stuffed Green Peppers, 72
Meatballs and Vegetables, 75
Beef and Broccoli Stir-Fry, 76
Skillet Rice and Chicken, 90
Tangy Turkey Spaghetti, 96
Lentil Soup, 108
Vegetable Beef Soup, 114
Lemon-Pepper Spinach, 121
Baked Tomatoes with
    Spinach, 123

FOLATE

Heart-Smart Function
Folate, also called folic acid, reduces levels of a blood chemical called homocysteine. Homocysteine plays a role in the narrowing of arteries and constriction of blood flow. Raising your intake of folate lowers your level of homocysteine.
RDA: 400 micrograms

Food Sources
Asparagus, broccoli, cabbage, dried beans and peas, lettuce, oranges, orange juice, spinach

Recipe/Page Number
Black-Eyed Peas and Rice, 57
Mexican Salad, 61
Spicy Vegetarian Tostadas, 62
Hearty Barley, 65
Pasta Primavera, 68
Beef and Broccoli Stir-Fry, 76
Red Beans with Ham, 80
Lemon-Pepper Spinach, 121

CALCIUM

Heart-Smart Function
Calcium is essential for the clotting of blood and for muscle and nerve function, and it may be important in controlling blood pressure.
RDA: 800 milligrams*

Food Sources
Dairy products, calcium-enriched orange juice, calcium-enriched rice, cereal grains, dried beans and peas, greens, sardines, salmon (bone-in)

Recipe/Page Number
Macaroni and Cheese, 63
Florentine Lasagna, 66
Chicken Quiche, 85
Turkey Chili Pie, 97

*The National Institutes of Health recommends 1,000 to 1,500 milligrams calcium per day for adults.

MAGNESIUM

Heart-Smart Function
Your body needs magnesium to process proteins and fats and to help the body turn food into fuel.
RDA: 350 milligrams

Food Sources
Green leafy vegetables, milk, nuts, seafood, whole grains

Recipe/Page Number
Catfish Gumbo, 42
Grouper Sandwiches, 43
Zesty Baked Salmon, 44
Greek-Style Snapper, 45

POTASSIUM

Heart-Smart Function
Potassium is important to a heart-healthy diet because of its relationship to sodium. A high intake of potassium can help offset sodium's tendency to raise blood pressure.
RDA: 800 milligrams

Food Sources
Apricots, bananas, cantaloupe, citrus fruits, citrus juices, greens, plums, potatoes, spinach, tomatoes

Recipe/Page Number
Roasted Pork Loin, 82
Blueberry-Melon Salad, 100
Vegetarian Chili, 113
Vegetable-Stuffed Yellow
  Squash, 122
Banana Ice Cream, 126

PHYTOCHEMICALS

Phytochemicals are natural plant chemicals that may protect you from heart disease. Some phytochemicals (like **carotenoids**) work as antioxidants; some influence hormone function. Phytochemicals are found in vegetables, fruits, whole grains, herbs, and spices, not supplements.

THE EATRIGHT PROGRAM

The EatRight program's emphasis on high-fiber, low-fat, and low-calorie foods makes the program an ideal tool for heart-healthy eating.

The EatRight program is based on a simple concept: Eat low-calorie, high-fiber foods that take a long time to eat and leave you feeling full, instead of high-calorie foods that take a short time to eat and provide more calories than you need before you've had time to feel full. For example, you could get 100 calories in 1 tablespoon of mayonnaise, which would take only a few seconds to eat. Or you could get those calories in a larger serving of a food that takes longer to eat: two apples or 5 cups of salad.

Unlimited Amounts

On the EatRight plan, you may have unlimited servings of fruits and vegetables, and liberal amounts of starchy foods such as whole grain breads and cereals, rice, and potatoes. Fats, oils, meats, and dairy foods are used in moderation, and you can still enjoy special occasion treats such as sweets and snack foods.

Instead of counting calories and fat grams, you can use the EatRight Food Guide (pages 24 and 25) to help you know what and how much to eat each day.

Special Needs

EatRight also is suitable for most people with **diabetes,** although those who take insulin should consult their physician and dietitian before beginning. Portions on the EatRight Food Guide are compatible with those of most diabetic eating plans. The EatRight plan meets the nutritional needs of most healthy people, so there's no need to take vitamin/mineral supplements. If you have **iron-deficiency anemia,** are **pregnant** or **breastfeeding,** see your physician before starting any eating program.

EatRight isn't a "special diet" that makes you sacrifice the foods you love. Instead, it's a lifetime plan that emphasizes delicious foods high in fiber, low in fat, and packed with vitamins and nutrients known to boost your heart's health. It gives you the tools to create a stronger, healthier heart while preserving the pleasures of eating and living well.

DIETARY GUIDELINES

The American Heart Association's dietary guidelines reflect the newest knowledge about diet and disease, and promote the same principles of healthy eating as the EatRight plan.

1. Eat a variety of foods. No single food can supply all of the nutrients in the amounts you need.

2. Balance the food you eat with physical activity to maintain or improve your weight.

3. Choose a diet with plenty of grain products, vegetables, and fruits.

4. Choose a diet low in fat, saturated fat, and cholesterol. No more than 30 percent of your total daily calories should come from fat.

5. Choose a diet moderate in sugars.

6. Choose a diet moderate in salt and other sodium. Too much sodium can raise blood pressure in certain people.

7. If you drink alcoholic beverages, do so in moderation. Though there is some evidence that moderate drinking may be associated with lower risk of heart disease in some people, too much alcohol has been linked to high blood pressure, stroke, certain cancers, and many other problems.

Zesty Baked Salmon (page 44)

HEART SMART RECIPES

The sample recipe below shows how you can use the recipes in this book to eat smart for your heart. The complete recipe for Florentine Lasagna is on page 66.

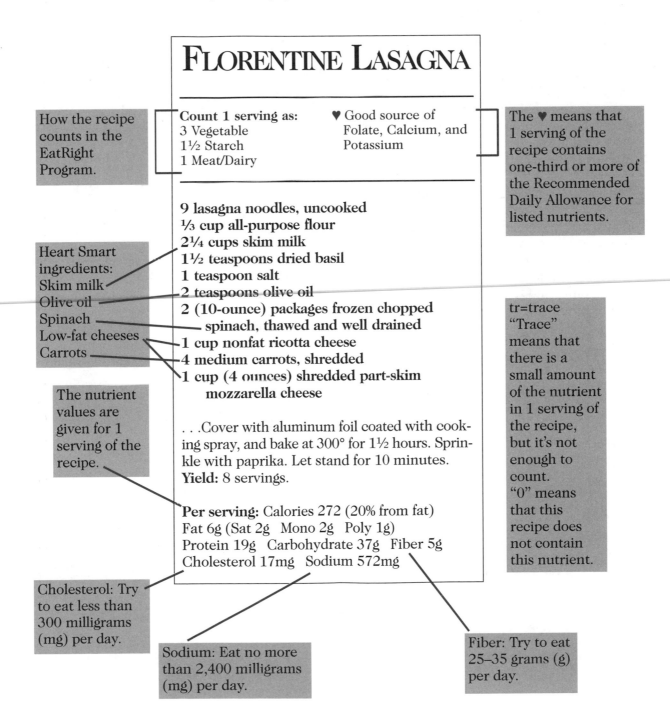

FLORENTINE LASAGNA

How the recipe counts in the EatRight Program.

Count 1 serving as:
3 Vegetable
1½ Starch
1 Meat/Dairy

♥ Good source of Folate, Calcium, and Potassium

The ♥ means that 1 serving of the recipe contains one-third or more of the Recommended Daily Allowance for listed nutrients.

Heart Smart ingredients:
Skim milk
Olive oil
Spinach
Low-fat cheeses
Carrots

9 lasagna noodles, uncooked
⅓ cup all-purpose flour
2¼ cups skim milk
1½ teaspoons dried basil
1 teaspoon salt
2 teaspoons olive oil
2 (10-ounce) packages frozen chopped spinach, thawed and well drained
1 cup nonfat ricotta cheese
4 medium carrots, shredded
1 cup (4 ounces) shredded part-skim mozzarella cheese

tr=trace "Trace" means that there is a small amount of the nutrient in 1 serving of the recipe, but it's not enough to count. "0" means that this recipe does not contain this nutrient.

The nutrient values are given for 1 serving of the recipe.

. . .Cover with aluminum foil coated with cooking spray, and bake at 300° for 1½ hours. Sprinkle with paprika. Let stand for 10 minutes.
Yield: 8 servings.

Per serving: Calories 272 (20% from fat)
Fat 6g (Sat 2g   Mono 2g   Poly 1g)
Protein 19g   Carbohydrate 37g   Fiber 5g
Cholesterol 17mg   Sodium 572mg

Cholesterol: Try to eat less than 300 milligrams (mg) per day.

Sodium: Eat no more than 2,400 milligrams (mg) per day.

Fiber: Try to eat 25–35 grams (g) per day.

Florentine Lasagna (page 66)

EATRIGHT FOOD GROUPS

The EatRight Program focuses on what you can eat, not what you can't.

The five EatRight Food Groups are lined up from left to right, starting with the Fat group (see the chart below). Most of the foods you eat should come from the right side of the chart (the Vegetable group and the Fruit group) while foods from the left side of the chart (Fat and Meat/Dairy groups) should be eaten less often. Look for the complete EatRight Food Guide, including food groups and serving sizes, on pages 24 and 25.

EATRIGHT FOOD CLASSIFICATIONS

In the EatRight program, foods are classified as **Preferred, Occasional,** or **Special Occasion. Preferred** foods are high-fiber and low-calorie, and take longer to eat, leaving you feeling fuller and more satisfied.

Occasional foods may have more calories and sodium and fewer nutrients due to refining or processing. For example, although ½ cup of orange juice counts as one fruit serving, juices are considered occasional foods on the EatRight plan. If you eat a fresh orange,

you'll get more fiber, and because the whole fruit takes longer to eat, you'll feel fuller. The EatRight plan allows up to two **Occasional** foods each day from each group for people who are not trying to lose weight.

Special Occasion foods are snacks and sweets you treat yourself to when the moment is right. Most are high in sugar, and many are high in fat and cholesterol. EatRight suggests a limit of 200 calories per week from **Special Occasion** foods.

NUMBER OF SERVINGS

In the chart below, notice that the Fat group has a maximum number of servings per day. The Meat/Dairy and Starch groups have a specific number of servings, and the Fruit and Vegetable groups each list minimum servings per day. Servings of vegetables and fruits are unlimited on the EatRight plan, and your goal is to eat more servings than the minimum. Use the EatRight Daily Servings Guide on the facing page to determine your daily servings.

EATRIGHT FOOD GROUPS

 Fat *
Maximum servings
per day: _____
45 calories/serving

Preferred: monounsaturated and polyunsaturated fats: olive oil, peanut oil, peanut butter, nuts, seeds, mayonnaise, salad dressings

Occasional: bacon, butter, gravy, margarine, sour cream

* Use all fats sparingly.

 Meat/Dairy
Specific servings
per day: _____
110 calories/serving

Preferred: fish, poultry (skin removed), skim milk, low-fat yogurt, low-fat cheeses

Occasional: lean cuts of beef, lamb, and pork; whole milk; cheese; eggs

 Starch
Specific servings
per day: _____
80 calories/serving

Preferred: whole grain breads, crackers, cereals, and pasta; brown rice; starchy vegetables: dried peas and beans, corn, potatoes, winter squash

Occasional: biscuits, white bread, regular crackers, white rice

EatRight Daily Servings Guide

Approximate Daily Calories	Fat (45 calories per serving)	Meat/Dairy (110 calories per serving)	Starch (80 calories per serving)	Fruit (60 calories per serving)	Vegetable (25 calories per serving)
1,200	3	3	5	4	4
1,400	3	3½	6	5	5
1,600	4	4	7	5	5
1,800	5	4	8	6	6
2,000	6	4	9	7	7
2,200	7	4½	10	8	8

The chart above shows the number of servings from each food group recommended at six calorie levels. To determine the total number of calories you need each day, multiply your current weight in pounds by one of the following factors:

Age 20 to 29: weight x 13=calories needed
Age 30 to 39: weight x 12=calories needed
Age 40 to 49: weight x 11=calories needed
Age 50 + : weight x 10=calories needed

The number you get from the previous formula is approximately the number of calories you need to maintain your current weight. For example, a 45-year-old woman who weighs 160 pounds would multiply her weight by 11. So she needs about 1,760 calories each day to maintain her weight.

If you need to lose weight, subtract 500 calories per day to lose a pound a week.

Fruit
Minimum servings per day: _____
60 calories/serving

Preferred: fresh and unsweetened frozen fruits

Occasional: juices, canned fruits, dried fruits

Vegetable
Minimum servings per day: _____
25 calories/serving

Preferred: fresh, frozen, and no-salt-added canned vegetables

Occasional: regular canned vegetables, vegetable juices, pickled vegetables (because they are high in sodium)

EATRIGHT FOOD GUIDE

Fat
45 calories per serving

Meat/Dairy
110 calories per serving

Starch
80 calories per serving

PREFERRED	SERVING SIZE
Avocado	1/8 medium
Mayonnaise	
regular	1 teaspoon
reduced-fat	1 tablespoon
Nuts, unsalted	
almonds	6
Brazil	2
cashews	6
peanuts	10
pecan halves	4
walnut halves	4
Oils	
canola, olive,	
peanut	1 teaspoon
Olives	8
Peanut butter	2 teaspoons
Salad dressings	
regular	1 tablespoon
reduced-fat	2 tablespoons
fat-free	3 tablespoons
Seeds, unsalted	
pumpkin, sesame,	
sunflower	1 tablespoon

OCCASIONAL

Bacon, cooked	1 slice
Bacon grease	1 teaspoon
Butter	
stick	1 teaspoon
whipped	2 teaspoons
reduced-fat	1 tablespoon
Coconut, sweetened	2 tablespoons
Cream	
half-and-half	2 tablespoons
sour, low-fat	3 tablespoons
sour, regular	2 tablespoons
whipping	1 tablespoon
nondairy	1 tablespoon
Cream cheese	
regular	1 tablespoon
reduced-fat	2 tablespoons
Fatback or saltpork	2 tablespoons
Gravy	2 tablespoons
Lard	1 teaspoon
Margarine	
regular stick, tub,	
or squeeze	1 teaspoon
reduced-fat	1 tablespoon
Shortening	1 teaspoon

PREFERRED	SERVING SIZE
Cheese	
low-fat or fat-free	3 ounces
reduced-fat	2 ounces
Parmesan, grated	1/4 cup
low-fat cottage or	
ricotta	3/4 cup
Egg whites	4 large
Egg substitute, plain	3/4 cup
Fish, fresh or frozen	3 ounces
Fish, canned	
salmon	3 ounces
sardines	4 medium
tuna, in water	3 ounces
tuna, in oil	2 ounces
Shellfish	
clams	15
crab, lobster, scallops	3 ounces
oysters	12 medium
shrimp	15 medium
Game, wild (skinned)	3 ounces
Poultry (skinned)	
chicken, turkey	
(white meat)	3 ounces
chicken, turkey	
(dark meat)	2 ounces
duck or goose	2 ounces
turkey breast, ground	3 ounces
Milk	
buttermilk, nonfat	1 cup
skim milk, 1/2% or 1%	1 cup
Yogurt, nonfat, plain	1 cup

OCCASIONAL

Beef, lean cuts	2 ounces
Cheese, 5 grams fat	
per ounce	1 1/2 ounces
Egg, whole	1
Lamb, roast, chop, leg	2 ounces
Soy milk	1 1/2 cups
Tofu	6 ounces or
	3/4 cup
Pork, lean cuts	2 ounces
Processed meats,	
low-fat	3 ounces
Veal, roast, chop	2 ounces

PREFERRED	SERVING SIZE
Bagel, whole grain	1/2
Bran, wheat	1/2 cup
Bread, whole grain	
regular	1 slice
reduced-calorie	2 slices
Cereal, dry, whole grain	1/2 cup
Cereal grains, cooked	1/2 cup
English muffin, whole	
grain	1/2
Pasta, whole grain	1/2 cup
Pita, whole grain,	
6" across	1/2
Popcorn, plain, popped,	
no fat added	3 cups
Rice, brown	1/3 cup
Rice cakes, whole grain	2
Vegetables	
dried beans and peas,	
cooked	1/3 cup
corn	
on cob	1 medium ear
kernels	1/2 cup
mixed vegetables	1 cup
peas, English	1/2 cup
potato, with skin	1 small
pumpkin	3/4 cup
squash, acorn, butternut	1 cup
sweet potato, plain	1/2 cup
Wheat germ	3 tablespoons

Special Occasion Foods

Limit: 200 calories per week
These Special Occasion Foods contain
100 calories (or less) and contain 2 grams
(or less) fat:

Angel food cake, unfrosted	1/16 cake
Cookies, fat-free	2
Fudgesicle, low-fat	1
Gelatin dessert	2/3 cup
Gingersnaps	4
Granola bar, low-fat	1 small
Hot cocoa mix	1 envelope
Ice cream, nonfat	1/2 cup
Popsicle	1
Pudding, nonfat	1/2 cup
Syrup, jam, jelly, honey	2 tablespoons
Yogurt, frozen, nonfat	1/2 cup
Vanilla wafers	4

Start eating right . . . Eat fewer foods on the left side of the chart . . . Eat more foods from the right . . . EatRight!

**Low-Calorie
High-Bulk
Slow-Eating**

Starch
(continued)

Fruit
60 calories per serving

Vegetable
25 calories per serving

Starch

OCCASIONAL	SERVING SIZE
Baked beans	1/3 cup
Biscuit, low-fat	1
Breadsticks	2 (4-inch)
Bread, white	1 slice
Bun, hot dog or hamburger	1/2
Cereal, dry, refined	3/4 cup
Cornbread, low-fat	1 (2-inch cube)
Crackers/snacks	
animal crackers	8
chips, low-fat	3/4 ounce
crackers, low-fat	8
graham	3 squares
Melba toast	4 slices
oyster crackers	24
pretzels	3/4 ounce
rice cakes	2 (4-inch)
saltine	6
Croutons, fat-free	1/2 cup
Granola, low-fat	1/4 cup
Muffin, low-fat	1 small
Pancake	1 (4-inch)
Pasta, cooked	1/2 cup
Potatoes, mashed	1/2 cup
Rice, white	1/3 cup
Roll, plain	1 small
Taco shell	1
Tortilla, corn or flour	1
Waffle, low-fat	1 (4-inch)

Fruit

PREFERRED	SERVING SIZE
Apple, small	1
Apricots, fresh	4
Banana, small	1
Blackberries	3/4 cup
Blueberries	3/4 cup
Cantaloupe	1 cup cubed
Cherries, sweet, fresh	12
Grapefruit, large	1/2
Grapes	15
Honeydew melon	1 cup cubed
Kiwifruit	1
Mango, small	1/2 fruit
Nectarine, small	1
Orange, small	1
Papaya	1 cup cubed
Peach, medium, fresh	1
Pear, small, fresh	1
Pineapple, fresh	3/4 cup
Plums, small	2
Raspberries	1 cup
Strawberries	1 1/4 cups
Tangerines, small	2
Watermelon	1 1/4 cups cubed

OCCASIONAL	
Applesauce (unsweetened)	1/2 cup
Apple, dried	4 rings
Apricot, canned	1/2 cup
Apricot, dried	8 halves
Cherries, canned	1/2 cup
Dates	3
Figs, dried	2
Fruit cocktail	1/2 cup
Fruit juices	
apple, grapefruit, orange, pineapple	1/2 cup
cranberry juice cocktail	
regular	1/3 cup
reduced-calorie	1 cup
fruit juice blends	1/3 cup
frozen fruit juice bar	1
grape, prune	1/3 cup
Grapefruit sections	3/4 cup
Mandarin oranges	3/4 cup
Peaches, pears, pineapple, canned	1/2 cup
Plums, canned	2
Prunes, dried	3
Raisins	2 tablespoons

Vegetable

PREFERRED	SERVING SIZE
Artichoke	1 medium
Asparagus	1/2 cup
Bamboo shoots	1/2 cup
Beans, green, wax	1/2 cup
Bean sprouts	1 cup
Beets	1/2 cup
Broccoli	1 cup raw or 1/2 cup cooked
Brussels sprouts	1/2 cup
Cabbage	1 cup raw or 1/2 cup cooked
Carrot	1 cup raw or 1/2 cup cooked
Cauliflower	1 cup raw or 1/2 cup cooked
Celery	1 cup raw
Cucumber	1
Eggplant	1/2 cup
Greens, cooked	1/2 cup
Kohlrabi	1/2 cup
Lettuce	1/4 head
Mushrooms	1 cup
Okra	6 pods or 1/2 cup
Onion	1/2 cup
Pea pods	1/2 cup
Peppers (all varieties)	1
Radishes	10
Rutabaga	1/2 cup cooked
Salad greens	1 cup
Scallions	1/2 cup
Spinach	1 cup raw or 1/2 cup cooked
Squash, summer	3/4 cup cooked
Tomato	1 small
Turnips	1/2 cup cooked
Water chestnuts	1/2 cup
Zucchini	3/4 cup cooked

OCCASIONAL	
Canned vegetables	1/2 cup
Pickle, dill	1 large
Sauerkraut	1/2 cup
Spaghetti sauce, low-fat	1/2 cup
Tomato juice	1/2 cup
Tomato paste	2 tablespoons
Vegetable juice	1/2 cup
Vegetables, pickled	1/2 cup

PORTION POWER

The EatRight Food Guide (pages 24 and 25) lists serving sizes in each food group so that you can track how much you eat from each group. For example, ½ cup cooked broccoli is one serving from the Vegetable group; one slice of whole grain bread is one 80-calorie serving from the Starch group. If you eat two slices of bread, you will count two servings from the Starch group; 1 cup of cooked broccoli would be two Vegetable servings.

Use a food scale to weigh portions of meat, poultry, and fish after cooking. To measure other foods, use standard measuring cups and spoons, and keep measures level.

After you've measured portions sizes for a while, you'll better be able to "eyeball" correct serving sizes. Use the guide below to help you approximate portion sizes.

Item	Equivalent Size
3 ounces cooked meat, poultry, or fish	Palm of small hand or 1 deck of cards
1 medium apple or orange	Tennis ball
1 teaspoon mayonnaise or margarine	Tip of thumb
1 serving low-fat cheese	1 (1-inch) cube

FLUID FACTS

As you consider your food selections, keep in mind that vegetables and fruits help meet your body's need for **water,** another important nutrient. Drink at least one glass of water with each meal and at least five more throughout the day. Avoid regular and diet soft drinks as well as coffee, tea, and other beverages containing caffeine. These drinks actually can increase your body's need for water.

THE ABCs OF LOW-FAT COOKING

The following EatRight principles of low-fat cooking are incorporated into the recipes in this book. Simply by enjoying the EatRight recipes, you're helping your heart stay healthy.

Cooking Methods
◆ Bake, broil, steam, and sauté foods in nonstick cookware coated with vegetable cooking spray.

Eggs
◆ Limit eggs to no more than four yolks a week.
◆ Be sure to count the eggs used in recipes.
◆ Use egg whites and egg substitutes.

Flavor
◆ Add flavor with herbs, spices, and flavored vinegars.
◆ Cook vegetables quickly in as little water as possible to preserve flavor and nutrients.

Meats
◆ Serve a smaller amount of meat and add another vegetable to the menu instead of planning a dinner around meat.
◆ Think of meat as a condiment or as a taste enhancer, and serve it in small amounts.
◆ Increase the amount of vegetables in a combination dish and reduce the amount of meat.
◆ Remove skin and visible fat from meats and poultry before serving.
◆ Roast meats and poultry on a rack so that the fat drips away. Baste with fat-free ingredients like fruit juice or wine.

Substitutions
◆ Substitute low-fat ingredients for high-fat items in your favorite high-fat recipes.

APPETIZERS

CHICK-PEA DIP

Count 1 serving as:
½ Starch

1 (15-ounce) can chick-peas, rinsed and
   drained
¼ cup chopped onion
1 tablespoon lime juice
1 teaspoon olive oil
¼ teaspoon black pepper
⅛ teaspoon salt
⅛ teaspoon ground red pepper
1 tablespoon chopped fresh parsley
1 medium tomato, chopped

Position knife blade in food processor bowl;
add chick-peas and next 6 ingredients.
Process until smooth. Stir in parsley and
tomato. Cover and chill. Serve with toasted
pita chips (chips not included in analysis).
Yield: 12 servings (serving size: 2 tablespoons).

Per serving: Calories 65 (18% from fat)
Fat 1g (Sat tr   Mono tr   Poly tr)
Protein 3g   Carbohydrate 11g   Fiber 2g
Cholesterol 0mg   Sodium 112mg

BLACK BEAN SALSA

Count 1 serving as:
1 Starch

1 (15-ounce) can black beans, rinsed
   and drained
¼ cup chopped green onions
1 tablespoon chopped fresh cilantro
1 tablespoon minced fresh jalapeño pepper
1 tablespoon lime juice
½ teaspoon ground cumin
⅛ teaspoon chili powder
1 large tomato, chopped
1 clove garlic, crushed

Combine all ingredients in a medium bowl,
stirring well. Cover and chill at least 2 hours.
Serve with no-oil-baked tortilla chips (chips
not included in analysis).
Yield: 10 (⅓-cup) servings.

Per serving: Calories 67 (5% from fat)
Fat tr (Sat tr   Mono tr   Poly tr)
Protein 4g   Carbohydrate 13g   Fiber 3g
Cholesterol 0mg   Sodium 104mg

Fresh Tomato Salsa

Count 1 serving as:
Free

2 large ripe tomatoes, chopped
¾ cup chopped green onions
½ cup chopped green pepper
½ cup finely chopped fresh parsley
1 tablespoon lemon juice
¼ teaspoon salt
¼ teaspoon hot sauce

Combine all ingredients in a medium bowl. Cover and chill. Serve with no-oil-baked tortilla chips (chips not included in analysis).
Yield: 12 (¼-cup) servings.

Per serving: Calories 11 (12% from fat)
Fat tr (Sat tr   Mono tr   Poly tr)
Protein tr   Carbohydrate 2g   Fiber 1g
Cholesterol 0mg   Sodium 57mg

Cauliflower Nuggets

Count 1 serving as:
1 Vegetable
½ Starch

♥ Good source of Vitamin C and Folate

½ cup water
1 medium head cauliflower, cut into
    48 bite-size pieces
1½ cups corn flake crumbs
⅓ cup all-purpose flour
⅓ cup whole wheat flour
½ teaspoon garlic powder
½ teaspoon ground cumin
½ teaspoon black pepper
⅛ teaspoon ground red pepper
3 egg whites
Vegetable cooking spray
¾ cup fat-free honey mustard dressing

Bring water to a boil in a saucepan. Add cauliflower; return to a boil. Cover, reduce heat to medium, and cook 5 minutes or until crisp-tender. Drain; let cool.

   Place crumbs in a heavy-duty, zip-top plastic bag; set aside. Combine flours and next 4 ingredients in a second zip-top plastic bag. Add cauliflower; shake to coat. Stir egg whites with a wire whisk until foamy; add cauliflower, tossing to coat. Add cauliflower to crumbs, and shake. Place on a baking sheet coated with cooking spray; coat cauliflower with cooking spray. Bake at 350° for 20 minutes or until lightly browned. Serve with dressing.
Yield: 12 servings.

Per serving: Calories 73 (12% from fat)
Fat 1g (Sat tr   Mono tr   Poly 1g)
Protein 3g   Carbohydrate 14g   Fiber 2g
Cholesterol 1mg   Sodium 188mg

SALMON CANAPÉS

Count 1 serving as:
½ Starch

1 (6¼-ounce) can salmon in water, drained
   and flaked
2 tablespoons minced onion
2 tablespoons minced celery
2 tablespoons low-fat mayonnaise
2 tablespoons low-fat sour cream
24 (2½- x 2- x ¼-inch) slices party
   rye bread
3 plum tomatoes, each cut into 8 slices
1 tablespoon chopped fresh parsley

Combine first 5 ingredients in a medium
bowl, stirring well. Spread 2 teaspoons salmon
mixture on each slice of bread; top each with
a tomato slice, and sprinkle with parsley.
Cover and chill.
Yield: 2 dozen (serving size: 1 canapé).

Per serving: Calories 43 (21% from fat)
Fat 1g (Sat tr   Mono tr   Poly tr)
Protein 3g   Carbohydrate 6g   Fiber 1g
Cholesterol 4mg   Sodium 121mg

CRUNCHY SNACK MIX

Count 1 serving as:
½ Starch

2 cups crisp wheat cereal squares
2 cups crisp corn cereal squares
2 cups crisp rice cereal squares
2 cups pretzel sticks
3 tablespoons Worcestershire sauce
1 tablespoon margarine, melted
1 tablespoon lemon juice
½ teaspoon garlic salt
½ teaspoon onion powder

Place first 4 ingredients in a 13- x 9- x 2-inch
pan. Combine Worcestershire sauce and remaining 4 ingredients, stirring well. Drizzle
Worcestershire sauce mixture over cereal
mixture, stirring well to coat. Bake at 250° for
45 minutes, stirring every 15 minutes. Let cool
completely, and store in an airtight container.
Yield: 24 (⅓-cup) servings.

Per serving: Calories 49 (13% from fat)
Fat 1g (Sat tr   Mono tr   Poly tr)
Protein 1g   Carbohydrate 10g   Fiber 1g
Cholesterol 0mg   Sodium 179mg

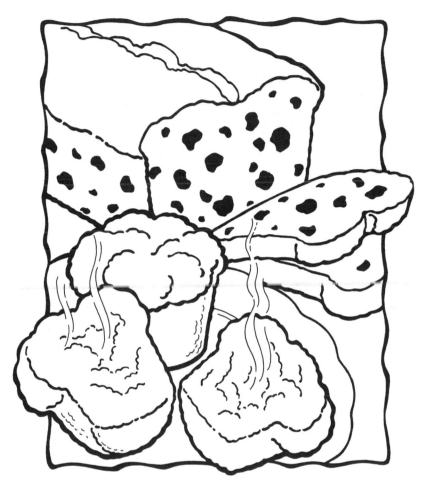

BREADS

CRISPY BISCUITS

Count 1 serving as:
1 Starch
½ Fat

2 cups plus 2 tablespoons all-purpose flour,
    divided
2½ teaspoons baking powder
¼ teaspoon salt
¾ cup skim milk
2 tablespoons vegetable oil
2 tablespoons plain nonfat yogurt

Combine 2 cups flour, baking powder, and salt
in a medium bowl, and stir well. Combine
milk, oil, and yogurt in a bowl; gradually add
to dry ingredients, stirring just until dry ingredients are moistened.
    Turn dough out onto surface sprinkled with
remaining 2 tablespoons flour, and knead
lightly 2 or 3 times. Pat dough to ½-inch
thickness; cut dough into rounds with a
floured 2¾-inch biscuit cutter. Place rounds
on an ungreased baking sheet. Bake at 450°
for 14 minutes or until lightly browned.
Yield: 1 dozen (serving size: 1 biscuit).

Per serving: Calories 108 (21% from fat)
Fat 3g (Sat tr   Mono 1g   Poly 1g)
Protein 3g   Carbohydrate 18g   Fiber tr
Cholesterol tr   Sodium 160mg

SAVORY ONION DROP BISCUITS

Count 1 serving as:
1 Starch
½ Fat

1 cup all-purpose flour
1 cup rye flour
1 teaspoon baking powder
½ teaspoon baking soda
¼ teaspoon salt
1¼ cups plain nonfat yogurt
¾ cup chopped green onions
2 tablespoons vegetable oil
1 teaspoon dried dillweed
¼ teaspoon pepper
Vegetable cooking spray

Combine first 5 ingredients in a medium bowl,
and stir well. Combine yogurt and next 4
ingredients in a bowl; add to dry ingredients,
stirring just until dry ingredients are moistened.
    Drop dough by tablespoonfuls onto a bak-
ing sheet coated with cooking spray. Bake at
425° for 12 to 15 minutes or until lightly
browned.
Yield: 1 dozen (serving size: 1 biscuit).

Per serving: Calories 111 (21% from fat)
Fat 3g (Sat tr   Mono 1g   Poly 1g)
Protein 4g   Carbohydrate 18g   Fiber 2g
Cholesterol tr   Sodium 164mg

GOLDEN CORNBREAD

Count 1 serving as:
1 Starch

¾ cup stone-ground yellow cornmeal
½ cup all-purpose flour
1 teaspoon baking powder
¼ teaspoon baking soda
¼ teaspoon salt
¾ cup skim milk
⅓ cup plain nonfat yogurt
Butter-flavored vegetable cooking spray

Combine first 5 ingredients in a medium bowl, and stir well. Combine milk and yogurt in a bowl; add to dry ingredients, stirring just until dry ingredients are moistened.

Pour batter into an 8-inch square pan coated with cooking spray. Bake at 425° for 20 to 22 minutes or until lightly browned. Cut into 9 squares, and serve warm.
Yield: 9 servings.

Per serving: Calories 80 (4% from fat)
Fat tr (Sat tr   Mono tr   Poly tr)
Protein 3g   Carbohydrate 16g   Fiber 1g
Cholesterol 1mg   Sodium 172mg

JALAPEÑO CORNBREAD

Count 1 serving as:
1 Starch

⅔ cup stone-ground yellow cornmeal
⅔ cup all-purpose flour
½ teaspoon baking soda
½ teaspoon salt
¼ cup (1 ounce) shredded reduced-fat sharp
    Cheddar cheese
¼ cup chopped onion
2 tablespoons chopped canned jalapeño
    pepper
⅔ cup nonfat buttermilk
2 tablespoons vegetable oil
2 egg whites, lightly beaten
Vegetable cooking spray

Combine first 4 ingredients in a bowl, stirring well. Stir in cheese, onion, and jalapeño pepper. Combine buttermilk, oil, and egg whites in a bowl; add to dry ingredients, stirring just until dry ingredients are moistened.

Pour batter into a 9-inch square pan coated with cooking spray. Bake at 425° for 20 minutes or until lightly browned. Cut into 12 (3- x 2¼-inch) pieces, and serve warm.
Yield: 12 servings.

Per serving: Calories 89 (30% from fat)
Fat 3g (Sat 1g   Mono 1g   Poly 1g)
Protein 3g   Carbohydrate 12g   Fiber 1g
Cholesterol 2mg   Sodium 202mg

APPLE-NUT MUFFINS

Count 1 serving as:
1 Starch
1 Fat

1 cup all-purpose flour
1 cup whole wheat flour
1½ teaspoons baking powder
½ teaspoon baking soda
¼ teaspoon salt
1 teaspoon ground cinnamon
⅓ cup firmly packed brown sugar
⅔ cup unsweetened apple juice
¼ cup unsweetened applesauce
¼ cup vegetable oil
1 teaspoon butter and nut flavoring
2 egg whites, lightly beaten
2 cups peeled, chopped apple
2 tablespoons chopped walnuts
Vegetable cooking spray

Combine first 6 ingredients in a bowl, and stir well; make a well in center of mixture. Combine brown sugar and next 5 ingredients in a bowl. Add to dry ingredients, stirring just until dry ingredients are moistened. Fold in apple and walnuts.

Spoon batter evenly into muffin pans coated with cooking spray. Bake at 400° for 20 to 22 minutes or until lightly browned. Remove from pans immediately.
Yield: 1½ dozen (serving size: 1 muffin).

Per serving: Calories 116 (30% from fat)
Fat 4g (Sat tr   Mono 2g   Poly 1g)
Protein 2g   Carbohydrate 19g   Fiber 2g
Cholesterol 0mg   Sodium 117mg

Recipe pictured on page 37.

CRANBERRY-ORANGE MUFFINS

Count 1 serving as:
1½ Starch

1½ cups all-purpose flour
½ cup whole wheat flour
1 tablespoon baking powder
¼ teaspoon salt
⅔ cup sugar
1 (16-ounce) can jellied whole-berry cranberry sauce
1 tablespoon grated orange rind
2 tablespoons vegetable oil
1 egg white, lightly beaten
Vegetable cooking spray

Combine first 5 ingredients in a large bowl, and stir well; make a well in center of mixture. Combine cranberry sauce and next 3 ingredients in a small bowl, stirring well. Add to dry ingredients, stirring just until dry ingredients are moistened.

Spoon batter evenly into muffins pans coated with cooking spray. Bake at 375° for 20 to 25 minutes or until lightly browned. Remove from pans immediately.
Yield: 1½ dozen (serving size: 1 muffin).

Per serving: Calories 133 (11% from fat)
Fat 2g (Sat tr   Mono 1g   Poly 1g)
Protein 2g   Carbohydrate 28g   Fiber 1g
Cholesterol 0mg   Sodium 124mg

Recipe pictured on page 37.

GLAZED LEMON-YOGURT MUFFINS

Count 1 serving as:
1 Starch

1 cup all-purpose flour
1 cup whole wheat flour
1 teaspoon baking powder
1 teaspoon baking soda
¼ teaspoon salt
1 cup plain nonfat yogurt
⅓ cup honey
¼ cup skim milk
1 tablespoon grated lemon rind
2 egg whites, lightly beaten
Vegetable cooking spray
2 tablespoons powdered sugar
2 tablespoons fresh lemon juice

Combine first 5 ingredients in a large bowl, and stir well; make a well in center of mixture. Combine yogurt and next 4 ingredients in a bowl, stirring well with a wire whisk. Add to dry ingredients, stirring just until dry ingredients are moistened.

Spoon batter evenly into muffin pans coated with cooking spray. Bake at 375° for 18 minutes or until lightly browned. Remove from pans. Combine powdered sugar and lemon juice, stirring with a wire whisk until sugar dissolves. Drizzle mixture over warm muffins.
Yield: 1½ dozen (serving size: 1 muffin).

Per serving: Calories 81 (3% from fat)
Fat tr (Sat tr   Mono tr   Poly tr)
Protein 3g   Carbohydrate 18g   Fiber 1g
Cholesterol tr   Sodium 148mg

PARMESAN TOAST

Count 1 serving as:
1 Starch

6 (1-ounce) slices French bread
Butter-flavored vegetable cooking spray
3 tablespoons freshly grated Parmesan
    cheese
¼ teaspoon garlic powder

Coat both sides of bread slices with cooking spray, and place bread on a baking sheet. Sprinkle bread evenly with cheese and garlic powder. Bake at 350° for 10 minutes or until bread is lightly toasted and cheese melts.
Yield: 6 servings.

Per serving: Calories 82 (20% from fat)
Fat 2g (Sat 1g   Mono tr   Poly tr)
Protein 4g   Carbohydrate 13g   Fiber 1g
Cholesterol 2mg   Sodium 204mg

APRICOT-WALNUT BREAD

Count 1 serving as:
1 Starch

1 cup all-purpose flour
½ cup whole wheat flour
½ cup regular oats, uncooked
2 teaspoons baking powder
⅓ cup sugar
⅓ cup finely chopped dried apricots
2 tablespoons coarsely chopped walnuts
¾ cup skim milk
¼ cup unsweetened applesauce
1 egg, lightly beaten
Vegetable cooking spray

Combine first 5 ingredients in a large bowl, and stir well. Stir in apricots and walnuts, and make a well in center of mixture. Combine milk, applesauce, and egg in a bowl; add to dry ingredients, stirring just until dry ingredients are moistened.

Pour batter into a 9- x 5- x 3-inch loafpan coated with cooking spray. Bake at 350° for 45 minutes or until a wooden pick inserted in center comes out clean. Let cool on a wire rack 10 minutes; remove from pan, and let cool completely on wire rack.
Yield: 16 servings.

Per serving: Calories 89 (12% from fat)
Fat 1g (Sat tr   Mono tr   Poly 1g)
Protein 3g   Carbohydrate 18g   Fiber 1g
Cholesterol 12mg   Sodium 71mg

BANANA-NUT BREAD

Count 1 serving as:
1 Starch
½ Fat

¾ cup all-purpose flour
¾ cup whole wheat flour
1 teaspoon baking powder
1 teaspoon baking soda
4 medium-size ripe bananas, peeled and mashed
2 egg whites, lightly beaten
⅓ cup honey
1 tablespoon vegetable oil
1 teaspoon butter and nut flavoring
Vegetable cooking spray
2 tablespoons chopped pecans

Combine first 4 ingredients in a medium bowl, and stir well; make a well in center of mixture. Combine banana and next 4 ingredients in a medium bowl, stirring well. Add to dry ingredients, stirring just until dry ingredients are moistened.

Pour batter into an 8½- x 4½- x 3-inch loafpan coated with cooking spray. Sprinkle pecans evenly on top of batter. Bake at 350° for 45 to 50 minutes or until a wooden pick inserted in center comes out clean. Remove from pan, and let cool completely on a wire rack.
Yield: 16 servings.

Per serving: Calories 104 (15% from fat)
Fat 2g (Sat tr   Mono 1g   Poly 1g)
Protein 2g   Carbohydrate 21g   Fiber 2g
Cholesterol 0mg   Sodium 117mg

*Apple-Nut Muffins (front) and
Cranberry-Orange Muffins (page 34)*

BLUEBERRY BREAD

Count 1 serving as:
1 Starch
½ Fat

1 cup all-purpose flour
1 cup whole wheat flour
2½ teaspoons baking powder
¼ teaspoon salt
⅓ cup sugar
1 cup skim milk
⅓ cup fat-free egg substitute
3 tablespoons vegetable oil
1 cup fresh or frozen blueberries, thawed
Vegetable cooking spray

Combine first 4 ingredients in a medium bowl, and stir well; make a well in center of mixture. Combine sugar, milk, egg substitute, and oil in a bowl, stirring well. Add to dry ingredients, stirring just until dry ingredients are moistened. Fold in blueberries.

Spoon batter into an 8½- x 4½- x 3-inch loafpan coated with cooking spray. Bake at 350° for 55 to 60 minutes or until a wooden pick inserted in center comes out clean. Remove from pan, and let cool completely on a wire rack.
Yield: 16 servings.

Per serving: Calories 105 (24% from fat)
Fat 3g (Sat tr   Mono 2g   Poly 1g)
Protein 3g   Carbohydrate 18g   Fiber 1g
Cholesterol tr   Sodium 127mg

HONEY-WHEAT BREAD

Count 1 serving as:
1 Starch

1 cup all-purpose flour
1 cup whole wheat flour
1 teaspoon baking powder
½ teaspoon baking soda
¼ teaspoon salt
1 cup nonfat buttermilk
⅓ cup honey
¼ cup fat-free egg substitute
Vegetable cooking spray

Combine first 5 ingredients in a bowl, and stir well; make a well in center of mixture. Combine buttermilk, honey, and egg substitute in a bowl. Add to dry ingredients, stirring just until dry ingredients are moistened.

Spoon batter into an 8½- x 4½- x 3-inch loafpan coated with cooking spray. Bake at 400° for 35 to 40 minutes or until a wooden pick inserted in center comes out clean. Remove from pan, and let cool completely on a wire rack.
Yield: 16 servings.

Per serving: Calories 83 (4% from fat)
Fat tr (Sat tr   Mono tr   Poly tr)
Protein 3g   Carbohydrate 18g   Fiber 1g
Cholesterol 1mg   Sodium 127mg

CREAM CHEESE-CHIVE ROLLS

Count 1 serving as:
1 Starch
½ Fat

1 (8-ounce) package nonfat cream cheese,
    softened
⅓ cup chopped fresh chives
2 tablespoons skim milk
1 package active dry yeast
¼ cup warm water (105° to 115°)
1 cup warm skim milk (105° to 115°)
⅓ cup sugar
¼ cup instant potato flakes
¼ cup vegetable oil
¾ teaspoon salt
1 egg white
4 cups all-purpose flour
Vegetable cooking spray

Combine cream cheese, chives, and 2 table-spoons milk in a bowl, and stir until well blended. Set aside.

Combine yeast and warm water; let stand 5 minutes. Combine yeast mixture, milk, and next 4 ingredients in a large bowl. Stir in egg white. Gradually stir in enough flour to form a stiff dough. Turn dough out onto a lightly floured surface, and knead until smooth and elastic (5 to 8 minutes).

Place dough in a bowl coated with cooking spray, turning to coat top. Cover and let rise in a warm place (85°), free from drafts, 1 hour or until doubled in bulk. Punch dough down; divide in half.

Roll each half into a 15- x 12-inch rectangle on a lightly floured surface. Spread each portion of dough with half of cream cheese mixture. Roll up dough jellyroll fashion, starting with long side. Cut each portion of dough into 15 (1-inch-thick) slices. Place slices on baking sheets coated with cooking spray. Cover and let rise in a warm place, free from drafts, 1 hour or until doubled in bulk. Bake at 350° for 17 to 20 minutes or until lightly browned.
Yield: 2½ dozen (serving size: 1 roll).

Per serving: Calories 97 (19% from fat)
Fat 2g (Sat tr   Mono 1g   Poly 1g)
Protein 3g   Carbohydrate 16g   Fiber 1g
Cholesterol tr   Sodium 111mg

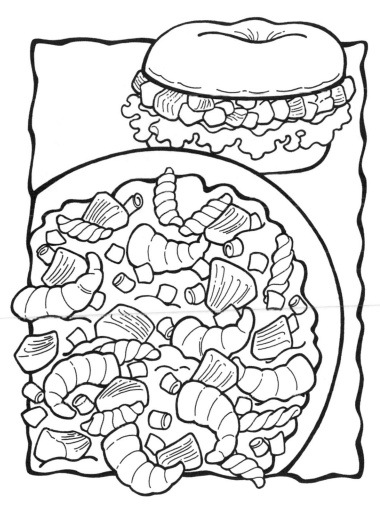

FISH & SHELLFISH

CATFISH GUMBO

Count 1 serving as:
1 Vegetable
1 Starch
1 Meat/Dairy

♥ Good source of Vitamin C, Folate, and Potassium

Vegetable cooking spray
2 cups chopped onion
1 large green pepper, diced
2 cloves garlic, minced
2 cups quick-cooking brown rice, uncooked
1 cup water
2 (28-ounce) cans no-salt-added tomatoes, undrained
1 (16-ounce) bag frozen okra
1 teaspoon dried basil
1 teaspoon hot sauce
½ teaspoon salt
½ teaspoon pepper
½ teaspoon dried thyme
1½ pounds farm-raised catfish fillets, cut into 1-inch pieces
½ cup cubed cooked lean ham

Coat a Dutch oven with cooking spray; place over medium-high heat until hot. Add onion, green pepper, and garlic; sauté until tender.

Add rice and next 8 ingredients; bring to a boil. Cover, reduce heat, and simmer 20 minutes. Add fish and cubed ham, and cook 10 minutes or until fish flakes easily when tested with a fork.
Yield: 9 (1½-cup) servings.

Per serving: Calories 210 (11% from fat)
Fat 3g (Sat 1g Mono 1g Poly 1g)
Protein 22g Carbohydrate 26g Fiber 6g
Cholesterol 50mg Sodium 326mg

VEGETABLE-TOPPED FLOUNDER

Count 1 serving as:
1 Vegetable
1 Meat/Dairy

♥ Good source of Vitamin C and Potassium

¾ cup sliced celery
2 tablespoons water
¼ teaspoon salt
1 small yellow squash, sliced
1 small zucchini, sliced
1 small onion, sliced
1 clove garlic, minced
2 medium tomatoes, chopped
¼ teaspoon dried basil
Dash of ground red pepper
4 (4-ounce) flounder fillets
Olive oil-flavored vegetable cooking spray
⅛ teaspoon chicken-flavored bouillon granules
⅛ teaspoon paprika

Combine first 7 ingredients in a saucepan; bring to a boil. Cover, reduce heat, and simmer 8 minutes or until vegetables are crisp-tender. Add tomato, basil, and pepper. Return to a boil; stir. Set aside, and keep warm.

Place fish in a baking dish coated with cooking spray. Sprinkle bouillon granules and paprika over fish. Bake at 400° for 12 minutes or until fish flakes easily when tested with a fork. To serve, top fish with vegetable mixture using a slotted spoon.
Yield: 4 servings.

Per serving: Calories 128 (11% from fat)
Fat 2g (Sat tr Mono tr Poly 1g)
Protein 21g Carbohydrate 7g Fiber 2g
Cholesterol 56mg Sodium 257mg

GROUPER SANDWICHES

Count 1 serving as:
2 Starch
1 Meat/Dairy

♥ Good source of
   Potassium

---

2 tablespoons low-fat mayonnaise
1 tablespoon sweet pickle relish
1 teaspoon grated onion
¼ teaspoon prepared horseradish
4 (4-ounce) grouper fillets
2 tablespoons nonfat buttermilk
⅓ cup corn flake crumbs
Vegetable cooking spray
¼ teaspoon lemon-pepper seasoning
4 (1½-ounce) whole wheat hamburger buns,
   toasted

Combine first 4 ingredients in a small bowl,
stirring well. Cover and chill.

Dip fish in buttermilk, and dredge in
crumbs. Place fish on a baking sheet coated
with cooking spray. Sprinkle evenly with
lemon-pepper seasoning. Bake at 425° for 10
minutes or until fish flakes easily when tested
with a fork.

Spread 1 tablespoon mayonnaise mixture
on bottom half of each bun. Top each with a
fish fillet and bun half, and serve warm.
Yield: 4 servings.

Per serving: Calories 267 (13% from fat)
Fat 4g (Sat 1g   Mono 1g   Poly 2g)
Protein 27g   Carbohydrate 31g   Fiber 3g
Cholesterol 60mg   Sodium 533mg

LEMON-GRILLED MAHIMAHI

Count 1 serving as:
1 Meat/Dairy
½ Fat

♥ Good source of
   Potassium

¼ cup fresh lemon juice
1 tablespoon low-sodium soy sauce
1 tablespoon olive oil
¼ teaspoon garlic powder
¼ teaspoon pepper
¼ teaspoon hot sauce
1 pound mahimahi fillets (or other firm
   white fish)
Vegetable cooking spray

Combine first 6 ingredients in a large heavy-
duty, zip-top plastic bag. Add fish; seal bag,
and shake gently until well coated. Marinate
in refrigerator 1 hour, turning bag occasionally. Remove fish from marinade, reserving
marinade. Place marinade in a small saucepan; bring to a boil. Remove from heat.

Place grill rack on grill over medium-hot
coals (350° to 400°). Arrange fish in a grill
basket coated with cooking spray. Place grill
basket on rack; grill, covered, 12 to 15 minutes or until fish flakes easily when tested
with a fork, turning once and basting with
reserved marinade.
Yield: 4 servings.

Per serving: Calories 144 (30% from fat)
Fat 5g (Sat 1g   Mono 3g   Poly 1g)
Protein 23g   Carbohydrate 2g   Fiber tr
Cholesterol 62mg   Sodium 253mg

OVEN-FRIED ORANGE ROUGHY

Count 1 serving as:
½ Starch
1 Meat/Dairy

♥ Good source of
   Potassium

---

4 (4-ounce) orange roughy fillets
¼ cup plain nonfat yogurt
⅓ cup fine, dry breadcrumbs
1 tablespoon freshly grated Parmesan cheese
½ teaspoon dried basil
⅛ teaspoon salt
Vegetable cooking spray

Coat fish with yogurt, and set aside. Combine breadcrumbs and next 3 ingredients in a shallow dish. Dredge fish in breadcrumb mixture. Place on a baking sheet coated with cooking spray. Coat fish lightly with cooking spray, and bake at 450° for 10 to 12 minutes or until fish flakes easily when tested with a fork. Broil 1 additional minute or until fish is lightly browned.
Yield: 4 servings.

Per serving: Calories 159 (14% from fat)
Fat 2g (Sat 1g Mono tr Poly 1g)
Protein 25g Carbohydrate 8g Fiber tr
Cholesterol 64mg Sodium 287mg

ZESTY BAKED SALMON

Count 1 serving as:
1 Meat/Dairy
1 Fat

♥ Good source of
   Potassium

---

1 pound salmon fillets
Vegetable cooking spray
2 tablespoons chopped green onions
1 tablespoon low-fat mayonnaise
1 tablespoon plain nonfat yogurt
1 teaspoon lemon-pepper seasoning
¼ teaspoon salt
¼ teaspoon dry mustard
Chopped green onions (optional)
Lemon slices (optional)

Place salmon, skin side down, in a baking pan coated with cooking spray. Bake at 425° for 18 minutes or until fish flakes easily when tested with a fork.

  Combine 2 tablespoons green onions and next 5 ingredients, and spread evenly over fish. Bake 2 additional minutes or until sauce is bubbly. To serve, transfer fish to serving plates. If desired, sprinkle with additional chopped green onions, and garnish with lemon slices.
Yield: 4 servings.

Per serving: Calories 164 (35% from fat)
Fat 6g (Sat 2g Mono 2g Poly 2g)
Protein 23g Carbohydrate 2g Fiber tr
Cholesterol 70mg Sodium 334mg

Recipe pictured on page 19.

GREEK-STYLE SNAPPER

Count 1 serving as:
1 Meat/Dairy
½ Fat

♥ Good source of
 Potassium

4 (4-ounce) red snapper fillets
Vegetable cooking spray
¼ cup lemon juice
1 tablespoon olive oil
½ teaspoon dried thyme
¼ teaspoon dried oregano
¼ teaspoon salt
¼ teaspoon pepper
¼ cup chopped green onions
1 clove garlic, minced

Place fish in a 13- x 9- x 2-inch baking dish coated with cooking spray. Combine lemon juice and next 5 ingredients; pour over fish. Top fish with green onions and garlic. Bake at 400° for 15 minutes or until fish flakes easily when tested with a fork. To serve, transfer to a serving platter, and drizzle with baking juices.
Yield: 4 servings.

Per serving: Calories 140 (31% from fat)
Fat 5g (Sat 1g   Mono 3g   Poly 1g)
Protein 22g   Carbohydrate 2g   Fiber tr
Cholesterol 60mg   Sodium 243mg

BAKED SOLE

Count 1 serving as:
1 Meat/Dairy

♥ Good source of
 Potassium

4 (4-ounce) sole fillets
2 tablespoons lemon juice
¼ cup fine, dry breadcrumbs
¼ teaspoon salt
¼ teaspoon pepper
¼ teaspoon dried basil
⅛ teaspoon garlic powder
Butter-flavored vegetable cooking spray

Brush fish with lemon juice, and set aside. Combine breadcrumbs and next 4 ingredients in a shallow dish. Dredge fish in breadcrumb mixture. Place fish in a 13- x 9- x 2-inch baking dish coated with cooking spray. Coat fish lightly with cooking spray. Bake at 450° for 12 minutes or until fish flakes easily when tested with a fork.
Yield: 4 servings.

Per serving: Calories 136 (12% from fat)
Fat 2g (Sat tr   Mono tr   Poly 1g)
Protein 23g   Carbohydrate 6g   Fiber tr
Cholesterol 62mg   Sodium 302mg

Sweet-and-Sour Swordfish

Count 1 serving as:	♥ Good source of
2½ Vegetable	Vitamin C and
1 Fruit	Potassium
1 Meat/Dairy	

1 pound swordfish fillets, cut into 2-inch
   pieces
1 (8-ounce) can pineapple chunks in juice,
   undrained
2 tablespoons low-sodium soy sauce, divided
Vegetable cooking spray
1 tablespoon plus 2 teaspoons cornstarch
1 cup water
¼ cup cider vinegar
1 (10-ounce) package frozen snow pea pods
½ cup thinly sliced carrot
1 tablespoon water
¼ cup canned sliced water chestnuts,
   drained
1 medium-size green pepper, cut into
   ½-inch strips
1 medium-size purple onion, cut into
   8 wedges and separated into pieces

Place fish in a large heavy-duty, zip-top plastic
bag. Drain pineapple, and reserve juice. Set
pineapple aside. Combine pineapple juice and
1 tablespoon soy sauce; add to fish. Marinate
in refrigerator 1 hour, turning bag occasionally. Drain fish, reserving marinade.

Coat a nonstick skillet with cooking spray;
place over medium-high heat until hot. Add
fish, and cook 10 minutes or until lightly
browned on all sides and fish flakes easily
when tested with a fork. Remove fish from
skillet; set aside, and keep warm.

Combine reserved marinade, remaining 1
tablespoon soy sauce, cornstarch, 1 cup water,
and vinegar in a small bowl, stirring well with
a wire whisk. Set aside.

Add snow peas, carrot, and 1 tablespoon
water to skillet; cover and cook over medium
heat 3 minutes. Increase heat to medium-
high; add water chestnuts, green pepper, and
onion. Stir-fry 1 minute. Add cornstarch mixture to vegetable mixture in skillet; add reserved pineapple. Stir-fry 2 minutes or until
thickened and bubbly. To serve, add fish to
vegetable mixture.
Yield: 4 servings.

Per serving: Calories 244 (21% from fat)
Fat 6g (Sat 2g   Mono 2g   Poly 2g)
Protein 23g   Carbohydrate 26g   Fiber 4g
Cholesterol 60mg   Sodium 365mg

TUNA SALAD ON BAGELS

Count 1 serving as:
1½ Starch
½ Meat/Dairy

1 (9-ounce) can tuna in water, drained
1 (8-ounce) can crushed pineapple in juice, drained
½ cup chopped celery
¼ cup low-fat mayonnaise
6 lettuce leaves
3 (4-inch) bagels, split into halves

Combine first 4 ingredients in a medium bowl, stirring well. Place 1 lettuce leaf on each bagel half; top each with ⅓ cup tuna mixture.
Yield: 6 servings.

Per serving: Calories 194 (7% from fat)
Fat 2g (Sat tr   Mono tr   Poly 1g)
Protein 15g   Carbohydrate 29g   Fiber 1g
Cholesterol 13mg   Sodium 326mg

GARLIC SAUTÉED SEAFOOD

Count 1 serving as:
1 Meat/Dairy

¼ cup plus 2 tablespoons lime juice
½ teaspoon dry mustard
¼ teaspoon salt
1⅓ pounds unpeeled medium-size fresh shrimp
1 pound orange roughy fillets
Vegetable cooking spray
3 cloves garlic, minced
¼ cup chopped fresh parsley
2 tablespoons chopped fresh chives

Combine first 3 ingredients in a small bowl, and set aside.
    Peel and devein shrimp; set aside. Cut fish fillets into 2-inch pieces. Coat a large nonstick skillet with cooking spray, and place over medium-high heat until hot. Add fish and garlic; sauté 2 minutes. Add shrimp, and sauté 3 additional minutes or until shrimp turn pink. Add lime juice mixture, parsley, and chives; cook 30 seconds, and remove from heat. Serve immediately.
Yield: 8 servings.

Per serving: Calories 109 (17% from fat)
Fat 2g (Sat tr   Mono tr   Poly tr)
Protein 20g   Carbohydrate 2g   Fiber tr
Cholesterol 98mg   Sodium 194mg

CURRIED SHRIMP AND PASTA SALAD

½ cup peeled, chopped cucumber
½ cup plain nonfat yogurt
½ cup low-fat sour cream
1 tablespoon lemon juice
¾ teaspoon salt
½ teaspoon curry powder
¼ teaspoon black pepper
¼ teaspoon paprika
⅛ teaspoon ground red pepper
1 clove garlic, crushed
¾ pound unpeeled medium-size fresh
    shrimp
2 cups water
1 (6-ounce) package rotini (spiral-shaped
    pasta), uncooked
1 medium-size sweet red pepper,
    chopped
2 green onions, chopped
2 (8-ounce) cans pineapple chunks in juice,
    drained
¼ teaspoon dried parsley flakes

Combine first 10 ingredients in a small bowl, stirring well. Cover cucumber mixture, and chill thoroughly.

Peel and devein shrimp. Place water in a medium saucepan. Bring water to a boil; add shrimp, and cook 3 to 5 minutes or until shrimp turn pink. Drain shrimp, and set aside.

Cook pasta according to package directions, omitting salt and fat. Rinse pasta in cold water, and drain well. Stir in sweet red pepper, green onions, pineapple chunks, and shrimp. Add chilled cucumber mixture, and toss to coat. Sprinkle pasta mixture with dried parsley flakes.
Yield: 6 (1⅓-cup) servings.

Per serving: Calories 230 (9% from fat)
Fat 2g (Sat 1g   Mono 1g   Poly tr)
Protein 13g   Carbohydrate 40g   Fiber 2g
Cholesterol 62mg   Sodium 393mg

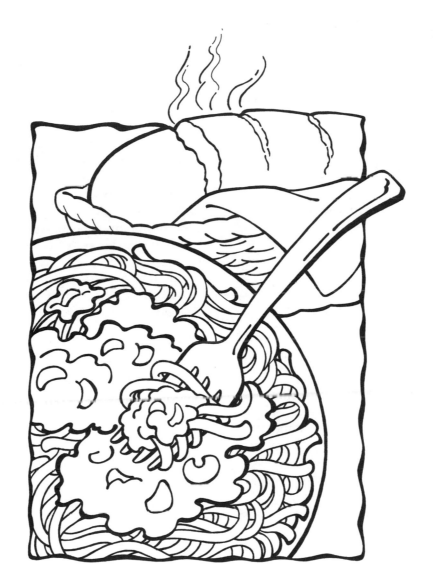

GRAINS
PASTAS &
LEGUMES

Chilled Couscous Salad

Count 1 serving as:
1 Vegetable
1 Starch

1 (10-ounce) package couscous, uncooked
1 teaspoon chicken-flavored bouillon granules
1⅓ cups boiling water
Yogurt Dressing
2 cups cherry tomatoes, halved
1 cup chopped green pepper
½ cup shredded carrot
1 medium cucumber, sliced

Combine uncooked couscous and chicken bouillon granules in a medium bowl. Add boiling water; cover mixture, and let stand 10 minutes or until liquid is absorbed. Let mixture cool slightly.

Add Yogurt Dressing, cherry tomatoes, chopped green pepper, shredded carrot, and sliced cucumber to cooled couscous; toss to coat. Cover and chill.
Yield: 12 (¾-cup) servings.

Yogurt Dressing

½ cup plain nonfat yogurt
¼ cup raspberry-flavored vinegar
2 tablespoons chopped onion
1 tablespoon water
1 tablespoon honey
1 teaspoon olive oil
¼ teaspoon dried basil
1 clove garlic, minced

Combine all ingredients in a small bowl, stirring well with a wire whisk. Cover and chill.
Yield: 1 cup.

Per serving: Calories 121 (6% from fat)
Fat 1g (Sat tr   Mono tr   Poly tr)
Protein 4g   Carbohydrate 24g   Fiber 2g
Cholesterol tr   Sodium 64mg

Mexican Bulgur

Count 1 serving as:
½ Vegetable
1½ Starch

♥ Good source of
Potassium

1 cup bulgur, uncooked
2½ cups boiling water
Vegetable cooking spray
½ cup chopped green pepper
½ cup chopped onion
1 clove garlic, minced
1 (16-ounce) can kidney beans, rinsed and
    drained
1 (14½-ounce) can whole tomatoes and
    green chiles, drained and chopped

Place bulgur in a medium bowl, and add boiling water. Cover and let stand 45 minutes or until water is absorbed.

  Coat a large nonstick skillet with cooking spray. Add green pepper, onion, and garlic, and sauté 2 minutes. Stir in bulgur, beans, and tomatoes; bring to a boil. Cover, reduce heat, and simmer 3 minutes or until liquid is absorbed.

Yield: 8 (¾-cup) servings.

Per serving: Calories 127 (4% from fat)
Fat 1g (Sat tr   Mono tr   Poly tr)
Protein 6g   Carbohydrate 26g   Fiber 7g
Cholesterol 0mg   Sodium 282mg

Curried Rice

Count 1 serving as:
½ Vegetable
½ Fruit
1 Starch
½ Fat

♥ Good source of
Vitamin C

1 tablespoon olive oil
1 cup broccoli flowerets
½ cup chopped sweet red pepper
½ cup chopped onion
¼ cup raisins
½ teaspoon salt
¼ teaspoon curry powder
⅛ teaspoon ground red pepper
⅛ teaspoon ground cumin
2 cups cooked brown rice (cooked without
    salt or fat)
1 (11-ounce) can mandarin oranges, drained

Heat oil in a large nonstick skillet over medium heat. Add broccoli and next 7 ingredients; sauté until broccoli is crisp-tender. Add cooked rice and oranges, and stir lightly. Cook over medium heat until thoroughly heated, stirring mixture often.

Yield: 7 (½-cup) servings.

Per serving: Calories 136 (17% from fat)
Fat 3g (Sat tr   Mono 2g   Poly tr)
Protein 3g   Carbohydrate 27g   Fiber 2g
Cholesterol 0mg   Sodium 175mg

FIESTA RICE

1 (4.4-ounce) package quick-cooking
    rice and pasta mix with Spanish-style
    seasonings
¾ cup quick-cooking brown rice, uncooked
1 cup chopped green pepper
1 cup chopped sweet red pepper
½ cup chopped onion
2½ cups water
⅛ teaspoon hot sauce

Combine all ingredients in a medium sauce-pan, and bring to a boil, stirring well. Cover, reduce heat, and simmer 5 minutes. Remove from heat, and let stand 5 minutes before removing cover. Serve warm.
Yield: 8 (½-cup) servings.

Per serving: Calories 135 (1% from fat)
Fat 1g (Sat tr   Mono tr   Poly tr)
Protein 3g   Carbohydrate 28g   Fiber 2g
Cholesterol 0mg   Sodium 240mg

GINGERED BROWN RICE

2½ cups water
1 cup brown rice, uncooked
1 cup chopped onion
¼ cup coarsely chopped dried cherries
1 tablespoon chopped fresh parsley
1 tablespoon peeled, minced gingerroot
½ teaspoon salt
1 tablespoon chopped fresh parsley

Bring water to a boil in a medium saucepan; add rice and next 5 ingredients. Cover, reduce heat, and cook 45 minutes or until rice is tender and liquid is absorbed. Top with 1 tablespoon parsley.
Yield: 7 (½-cup) servings.

Per serving: Calories 119 (6% from fat)
Fat 1g (Sat tr   Mono tr   Poly tr)
Protein 3g   Carbohydrate 26g   Fiber 2g
Cholesterol 0mg   Sodium 172mg

SAVORY BROWN RICE

Count 1 serving as:
1½ Starch

⅔ cup brown rice, uncooked
⅔ cup chopped celery
⅓ cup chopped onion
1⅔ cups water
¾ teaspoon chicken-flavored bouillon
    granules
¼ teaspoon dried parsley flakes
¼ teaspoon pepper

Combine all ingredients in a medium saucepan. Bring to a boil; cover, reduce heat, and simmer 50 minutes or until rice is tender and liquid is absorbed.
Yield: 4 (½-cup) servings.

Per serving: Calories 127 (7% from fat)
Fat 1g (Sat tr   Mono tr   Poly tr)
Protein 3g   Carbohydrate 26g   Fiber 2g
Cholesterol tr   Sodium 262mg

YELLOW AND BROWN RICE

Count 1 serving as:
2 Starch

3⅓ cups water
1 (5-ounce) package saffron-seasoned
    yellow rice mix
2 cups quick-cooking brown rice, uncooked

Bring water to a boil in a medium saucepan. Add yellow rice mix. Cover, reduce heat, and simmer 10 minutes. Add brown rice, and stir. Cover and simmer 5 additional minutes. Remove from heat, and let stand 5 minutes. Fluff with a fork before serving.
Yield: 12 (½-cup) servings.

Per serving: Calories 155 (6% from fat)
Fat 1g (Sat tr   Mono tr   Poly tr)
Protein 4g   Carbohydrate 33g   Fiber 2g
Cholesterol tr   Sodium 207mg

PARMESAN FETTUCCINE

Count 1 serving as:
1½ Starch
1 Fat

8 ounces fettuccine, uncooked
2 tablespoons skim milk
1 teaspoon poppy seeds
¼ teaspoon garlic salt
½ cup freshly grated Parmesan cheese

Cook pasta according to package directions, omitting salt and fat. Drain; set aside, and keep warm.

Combine milk, poppy seeds, and garlic salt in a small saucepan; cook over low heat until thoroughly heated (do not boil). Add pasta, and stir lightly. Add cheese, and toss well.
Yield: 6 (⅔-cup) servings.

Per serving: Calories 174 (22% from fat)
Fat 4g (Sat 2g   Mono 1g   Poly 1g)
Protein 8g   Carbohydrate 25g   Fiber 1g
Cholesterol 39mg   Sodium 205mg

LINGUINE WITH MARINARA SAUCE

Count 1 serving as:
2 Vegetable
1½ Starch

♥ Good source of Vitamin C and Potassium

Olive oil-flavored vegetable cooking spray
1 cup chopped onion
½ cup chopped green pepper
½ cup shredded carrot
½ cup sliced celery
2 cloves garlic, minced
3 cups peeled, chopped tomato
1 (6-ounce) can tomato paste
1½ teaspoons dried basil
½ teaspoon dried oregano
½ teaspoon salt
½ teaspoon sugar
⅛ teaspoon pepper
8 ounces linguine, uncooked

Coat a nonstick skillet with cooking spray; place over medium-high heat until hot. Add onion and next 4 ingredients; sauté 5 minutes or until tender. (Add water, 1 tablespoon at a time, if needed to tenderize vegetables.) Add tomato and next 6 ingredients; bring to a boil. Cover, reduce heat, and simmer 45 minutes.

Cook pasta according to package directions, omitting salt and fat. Drain. To serve, spoon sauce over pasta.
Yield: 8 servings (serving size: ½ cup pasta and ½ cup sauce).

Per serving: Calories 174 (6% from fat)
Fat 1g (Sat tr   Mono tr   Poly tr)
Protein 6g   Carbohydrate 37g   Fiber 4g
Cholesterol 0mg   Sodium 365mg

ZESTY CHILLED ORZO

Count 1 serving as:
1½ Starch

¾ cup orzo, uncooked
½ cup chopped celery
½ cup chopped green pepper
⅓ cup chopped purple onion
2 tablespoons raspberry-flavored vinegar
1 teaspoon olive oil
½ teaspoon salt
½ teaspoon dried thyme

Cook orzo according to package directions, omitting salt and fat. Drain.

Combine orzo, celery, pepper, and onion in a medium bowl. Combine vinegar and remaining 3 ingredients, and pour over orzo mixture. Toss lightly. Cover and chill at least 1 hour.
Yield: 4 (¾-cup) servings.

Per serving: Calories 120 (12% from fat)
Fat 2g (Sat tr   Mono 1g   Poly tr)
Protein 4g   Carbohydrate 23g   Fiber 2g
Cholesterol 0mg   Sodium 305mg

BLACK-EYED PEAS AND RICE

Count 1 serving as: ♥ Good source of
1 Vegetable   Vitamin C, Folate,
1½ Starch   and Potassium

Olive oil-flavored vegetable cooking spray
1 cup chopped green pepper
1 cup chopped sweet red pepper
½ cup finely chopped celery
¼ cup shredded carrot
2 tablespoons water
½ teaspoon salt
½ teaspoon Worcestershire sauce
¼ teaspoon black pepper
⅛ teaspoon ground red pepper
2 cloves garlic, minced
2 cups cooked brown rice (cooked without salt or fat)
1 (16-ounce) can black-eyed peas, drained
1 cup chopped green onions

Coat a large nonstick skillet with cooking spray; place over medium-high heat until hot. Add green pepper and next 9 ingredients; sauté until vegetables are tender. Stir in cooked rice and peas. Top with green onions, and serve warm.
Yield: 8 (⅔-cup) servings.

Per serving: Calories 138 (6% from fat)
Fat 1g (Sat tr   Mono tr   Poly tr)
Protein 6g   Carbohydrate 27g   Fiber 6g
Cholesterol 0mg   Sodium 296mg

Zesty Chilled Orzo

Rice and Bean Casserole

Count 1 serving as:
3 Starch
½ Meat/Dairy

♥ Good source of
Folate and Potassium

Vegetable cooking spray
1 cup chopped onion
½ cup chopped green pepper
3 cups cooked brown rice (cooked without salt or fat)
1 (16-ounce) can pinto beans, rinsed and drained
¼ cup sliced ripe olives
3 tablespoons chopped canned jalapeño pepper
¼ teaspoon salt
Vegetable cooking spray
1 cup (4 ounces) shredded reduced-fat sharp Cheddar cheese

Coat a large nonstick skillet with cooking spray; place over medium-high heat until hot. Add onion and green pepper; sauté 5 minutes or until tender. Stir in rice and next 4 ingredients. Spoon mixture into a 1-quart baking dish coated with cooking spray. Bake at 350° for 20 minutes or until thoroughly heated. Top with cheese, and bake 5 additional minutes or until cheese melts.
Yield: 6 (¾-cup) servings.

Per serving: Calories 291 (16% from fat)
Fat 5g (Sat 2g   Mono 2g   Poly 1g)
Protein 15g   Carbohydrate 47g   Fiber 9g
Cholesterol 10mg   Sodium 483mg

Baked Navy Beans and Corn

Count 1 serving as:
2 Starch

♥ Good source of
Folate and Potassium

1 (16-ounce) can navy beans, rinsed and drained
2 cups frozen whole-kernel corn, thawed
½ cup chopped purple onion
½ cup chopped green pepper
1 tablespoon brown sugar
3 tablespoons ketchup
1 tablespoon cider vinegar
1 teaspoon Worcestershire sauce
½ teaspoon dry mustard
Vegetable cooking spray

Combine first 9 ingredients in a 1-quart baking dish coated with cooking spray; stir well. Cover and bake at 350° for 45 minutes or until thoroughly heated.
Yield: 7 (½-cup) servings.

Per serving: Calories 150 (4% from fat)
Fat 1g (Sat tr   Mono tr   Poly tr)
Protein 7g   Carbohydrate 31g   Fiber 6g
Cholesterol 0mg   Sodium 240mg

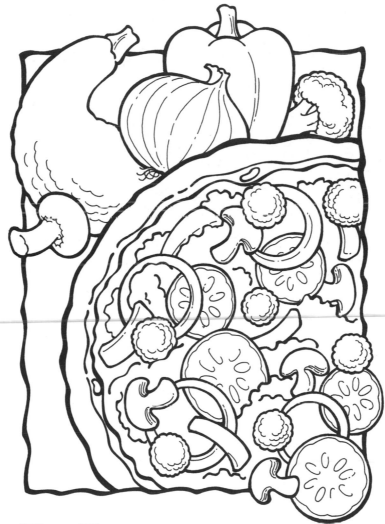

MEATLESS MAIN DISHES

BLACK BEAN PIE

Count 1 serving as:
1 Vegetable
2 Starch
½ Meat/Dairy

♥ Good source of
Vitamin C, Folate,
and Potassium

2½ cups frozen shredded hash brown
  potatoes, thawed
3 cups Fresh Tomato Salsa, divided
  (page 29)
1 (15-ounce) can black beans, rinsed and
  drained
1 tablespoon canned chopped jalapeño
  pepper
½ teaspoon cumin seeds
1 cup (4 ounces) shredded reduced-fat
  sharp Cheddar cheese

Press potato into bottom and up sides of a
9-inch pieplate. Bake at 400° for 20 minutes
or until edges are lightly browned. Remove
from oven, and set aside.

  Combine 1½ cups Fresh Tomato Salsa,
beans, pepper, and cumin seeds in a medium
bowl. Spoon into prepared potato shell. Top
with cheese. Bake at 350° for 25 minutes. Remove from oven, and let stand 5 minutes. Cut
into 6 wedges. To serve, top each wedge with
¼ cup salsa.
Yield: 6 servings.

Per serving: Calories 249 (15% from fat)
Fat 4g (Sat 2g Mono 1g Poly tr)
Protein 14g Carbohydrate 41g Fiber 8g
Cholesterol 10mg Sodium 414mg

BLACK BEAN PATTIES WITH FRESH TOMATO SALSA

Count 1 serving as:
1 Vegetable
2½ Starch
½ Fat

♥ Good source of
Folate and Potassium

1 (15-ounce) can black beans, rinsed and
  drained
¼ cup all-purpose flour
¼ cup finely chopped onion
2 teaspoons dried parsley flakes
¼ teaspoon pepper
⅛ teaspoon dried rosemary
⅛ teaspoon dried thyme
⅛ teaspoon dried cilantro
1 egg white
1 clove garlic, finely chopped
1 tablespoon olive oil
¾ cup Fresh Tomato Salsa (page 29)

Place beans in a medium bowl, and mash with
a fork. Add flour and next 8 ingredients, stirring well. Shape bean mixture into 4 patties.

  Heat oil in a large nonstick skillet over
medium heat. Add patties, and cook until
lightly browned on both sides, turning once.
To serve, top each patty with 3 tablespoons
Fresh Tomato Salsa.
Yield: 4 servings.

Per serving: Calories 237 (15% from fat)
Fat 4g (Sat 1g Mono 3g Poly tr)
Protein 12g Carbohydrate 39g Fiber 9g
Cholesterol 0mg Sodium 325mg

PINTO BEAN AND CORNBREAD BAKE

Count 1 serving as:
1 Vegetable
3½ Starch

♥ Good source of Folate and Potassium

2 (16-ounce) cans pinto beans, rinsed and drained
1 cup chopped onion
⅔ cup stone-ground cornmeal
⅔ cup all-purpose flour
½ teaspoon baking soda
¼ teaspoon salt
⅔ cup nonfat buttermilk
¼ cup fat-free egg substitute
2 tablespoons water
1 (8¾-ounce) can no-salt-added whole-kernel corn, drained
1 tablespoon canned chopped jalapeño pepper
2 medium tomatoes, sliced

Combine beans and onion in an 11- x 7- x 1½-inch baking dish, and set aside.
Combine cornmeal and next 3 ingredients in a medium bowl. Combine buttermilk, egg substitute, and water, stirring well. Add milk mixture to dry ingredients, stirring just until dry ingredients are moistened. Stir in corn and jalapeño pepper. Pour batter over bean mixture (do not stir).
Bake at 350° for 30 minutes or until cornbread is lightly browned. Cut into 8 servings, and top servings evenly with tomato slices.
Yield: 8 servings.

Per serving: Calories 286 (4% from fat)
Fat 1g (Sat tr   Mono tr   Poly tr)
Protein 14g   Carbohydrate 56g   Fiber 12g
Cholesterol 1mg   Sodium 471mg

MEXICAN SALAD

Count 1 serving as:
2 Vegetable
3 Starch
1 Fat

♥ Good source of Vitamin C, Folate, and Potassium

1 cup chopped onion
1 cup sliced celery
1 (15-ounce) can black beans, rinsed and drained
1 (15-ounce) can no-salt-added whole-kernel corn, drained
1 (4½-ounce) can chopped green chiles
4 medium tomatoes, chopped
2 large green peppers, seeded and chopped
⅓ cup cider vinegar
2 teaspoons chili powder
1½ teaspoons ground cumin
2 teaspoons vegetable oil
8 cups shredded lettuce
1 cup (4 ounces) shredded reduced-fat sharp Cheddar cheese
1 (8-ounce) package no-oil-baked tortilla chips

Combine first 7 ingredients in a large bowl. Combine vinegar and next 3 ingredients in a small bowl; pour over corn mixture, and toss to coat. Cover and chill at least 1 hour.
To serve, spoon vegetable mixture over lettuce, and top with cheese. Place tortilla chips around salad.
Yield: 8 servings.

Per serving: Calories 324 (16% from fat)
Fat 6g (Sat 2g   Mono 2g   Poly 1g)
Protein 15g   Carbohydrate 57g   Fiber 10g
Cholesterol 8mg   Sodium 570mg

Spicy Vegetarian Tostadas

Count 1 serving as:
1 Vegetable
2½ Starch
½ Meat/Dairy

♥ Good source of Vitamin C, Folate, and Potassium

1 (16-ounce) can red beans, rinsed, drained, and divided
1 (15-ounce) can no-salt-added whole-kernel corn, drained
1 (14½-ounce) can whole tomatoes and green chiles
½ cup chopped green pepper
½ cup chopped onion
1½ teaspoons chili powder
6 (7-inch) corn tortillas
3 cups shredded lettuce
2 medium tomatoes, chopped
¾ cup (3 ounces) shredded reduced-fat sharp Cheddar cheese
¾ cup plain nonfat yogurt

Place 1 cup beans in a shallow bowl, and mash with a fork. Place in a medium sauce-pan, and add remaining beans, corn, and next 4 ingredients. Bring to a boil; cover, reduce heat, and simmer 10 minutes. Uncover and cook until thickened and bubbly, stirring occasionally. Set aside, and keep warm.

Place tortillas in a single layer on a baking sheet; bake at 350° for 10 minutes or until crisp. Spread bean mixture evenly on tortillas. Top with lettuce, chopped tomato, and cheese. Top each with 2 tablespoons yogurt.
Yield: 6 servings.

Per serving: Calories 271 (14% from fat)
Fat 4g (Sat 2g   Mono 1g   Poly 1g)
Protein 15g   Carbohydrate 48g   Fiber 9g
Cholesterol 8mg   Sodium 526mg

Breakfast Burritos

Count 1 serving as:
½ Vegetable
1½ Starch
½ Meat/Dairy

Butter-flavored vegetable cooking spray
½ cup frozen chopped onion, celery, and pepper blend, thawed
¼ teaspoon ground cumin
Dash of ground red pepper
1 cup fat-free egg substitute
4 (7-inch) fat-free flour tortillas
¼ cup (1 ounce) shredded reduced-fat sharp Cheddar cheese
¼ cup salsa

Coat a medium nonstick skillet with cooking spray; place over medium-high heat until hot. Add vegetable blend, and sauté until tender. Add cumin and ground red pepper, stirring well. Add egg substitute; cook over medium heat until egg is set, stirring occasionally.

Microwave tortillas at HIGH 45 seconds or until thoroughly heated. Spoon egg mixture evenly onto centers of tortillas. Top each portion of egg mixture with 1 tablespoon cheese. Fold tortillas in half, and top each with 1 tablespoon salsa.
Yield: 4 servings.

Per serving: Calories 186 (21% from fat)
Fat 4g (Sat 1g   Mono 2g   Poly 1g)
Protein 10g   Carbohydrate 27g   Fiber 2g
Cholesterol 4mg   Sodium 344mg

French Toast with Strawberries

Count 1 serving as:
½ Fruit
1 Starch

♥ Good source of Vitamin C

½ cup fat-free egg substitute
½ cup skim milk
½ teaspoon vanilla extract
6 (1-ounce) slices whole wheat bread
Butter-flavored vegetable cooking spray
2 tablespoons powdered sugar, sifted
1½ cups sliced fresh strawberries

Combine first 3 ingredients in a shallow bowl, stirring well with a wire whisk. Dip each bread slice in egg mixture, and place on a baking sheet coated with cooking spray. Bake at 425° for 15 to 17 minutes or until lightly browned. Remove from oven, and sprinkle evenly with sugar. Top each slice with ¼ cup strawberries.
Yield: 6 servings.

Per serving: Calories 106 (12% from fat)
Fat 1g (Sat tr   Mono 1g   Poly tr)
Protein 5g   Carbohydrate 20g   Fiber 3g
Cholesterol tr   Sodium 181mg

Macaroni and Cheese

Count 1 serving as:
2 Starch
1 Meat/Dairy

♥ Good source of Calcium

2½ cups elbow macaroni, uncooked
1 cup skim milk
½ teaspoon salt
¼ teaspoon hot sauce
1 egg
1 egg white
Butter-flavored vegetable cooking spray
1½ cups (6 ounces) shredded reduced-fat
    sharp Cheddar cheese
¼ teaspoon paprika

Cook macaroni according to package directions, omitting salt and fat. Drain and set aside.

Combine milk and next 4 ingredients in a medium bowl, stirring well with a wire whisk; set aside. Spoon half of macaroni into a 1½-quart baking dish coated with cooking spray. Sprinkle half of cheese over macaroni. Add remaining macaroni and milk mixture (do not stir). Top with remaining cheese, and sprinkle with paprika. Bake at 350° for 40 minutes or until set.
Yield: 6 (1-cup) servings.

Per serving: Calories 274 (22% from fat)
Fat 7g (Sat 4g   Mono 2g   Poly 1g)
Protein 16g   Carbohydrate 36g   Fiber 2g
Cholesterol 51mg   Sodium 390mg

Mexican Corn Casseroles

Count 1 serving as:
½ Vegetable
1½ Starch
½ Meat/Dairy

1 (15-ounce) can no-salt-added whole-kernel
   corn, drained
1 (4½-ounce) can chopped green chiles,
   drained
¼ cup chopped green pepper
Butter-flavored vegetable cooking spray
1 cup skim milk
½ cup fat-free egg substitute
2 tablespoons stone-ground cornmeal
¼ teaspoon salt
1½ cups (6 ounces) shredded part-skim
   mozzarella cheese, divided
1 medium tomato, chopped
12 no-oil-baked tortilla chips

Combine first 3 ingredients in a medium
bowl; spoon evenly into 6 (1-cup) ovenproof
baking dishes coated with cooking spray.
Combine milk, egg substitute, cornmeal, and
salt in a medium bowl, stirring well with a
wire whisk. Pour ¼ cup milk mixture into
each dish, and top evenly with 1 cup cheese.

   Place dishes on a baking sheet, and bake at
350° for 30 minutes. Top evenly with tomato
and remaining ½ cup cheese. Bake 5 additional minutes or until cheese melts. Place 2
tortilla chips on side of each dish.
Yield: 6 servings.

Per serving: Calories 180 (27% from fat)
Fat 5g (Sat 3g Mono 2g Poly tr)
Protein 13g Carbohydrate 23g Fiber 3g
Cholesterol 16mg Sodium 321mg

Mushroom-Spinach Casserole

Count 1 serving as:
2 Vegetable
1 Meat/Dairy
½ Fat

1 (16-ounce) package frozen chopped
   spinach, thawed
1 cup soft whole wheat breadcrumbs
1 cup fat-free egg substitute
1 tablespoon dried onion flakes
1 teaspoon lemon-pepper seasoning
1 pound fresh mushrooms, sliced
1 (24-ounce) carton 1% low-fat cottage
   cheese
2 cups (8 ounces) shredded reduced-fat
   sharp Cheddar cheese, divided
Vegetable cooking spray

Place spinach on paper towels, and press to
remove excess moisture. Set aside. Combine
breadcrumbs and next 3 ingredients in a large
bowl. Add spinach, mushrooms, cottage
cheese, and 1½ cups Cheddar cheese, stirring
well to combine.

   Place spinach mixture in a 13- x 9- x 2-inch
baking dish coated with cooking spray. Bake,
uncovered, at 350° for 40 minutes. Sprinkle
with remaining ½ cup Cheddar cheese; bake
5 additional minutes or until cheese melts.
Yield: 8 servings.

Per serving: Calories 196 (29% from fat)
Fat 6g (Sat 4g Mono 2g Poly tr)
Protein 23g Carbohydrate 12g Fiber 3g
Cholesterol 19mg Sodium 578mg

Hearty Barley

Count 1 serving as:
2 Vegetable
2½ Fruit
1 Starch
½ Meat/Dairy

♥ Good source of Vitamin C, Folate, and Potassium

2 cups water
1 cup barley, uncooked
1 (15-ounce) can black beans, rinsed and drained
1 (8-ounce) can pineapple chunks in juice, drained
1½ cups broccoli flowerets
1 cup chopped sweet red pepper
1 cup chopped green pepper
1 cup cubed cantaloupe
½ cup chopped celery
Pineapple-Honey Mustard Dressing (page 106)
3 tablespoons chopped, dry roasted, unsalted peanuts

Bring 2 cups water to a boil in a medium saucepan. Add barley; cover, reduce heat, and simmer 10 to 12 minutes or until barley is tender. Remove from heat; let stand, covered, 5 minutes. Place saucepan with barley in a pan of cold water, and let cool to room temperature. Drain barley.

   Combine barley, beans, and next 6 ingredients in a large bowl. Add Pineapple-Honey Mustard Dressing, and toss lightly to coat. Top with peanuts.
Yield: 6 (1½-cup) servings.

Per serving: Calories 332 (9% from fat)
Fat 3g (Sat 1g   Mono 1g   Poly 1g)
Protein 12g   Carbohydrate 68g   Fiber 12g
Cholesterol 0mg   Sodium 515mg

Vegetable Medley on Orzo

Count 1 serving as:
2 Vegetable
1½ Starch

♥ Good source of Potassium

1 cup sliced carrot
1 cup canned Oriental broth, undiluted and divided
2 tablespoons low-sodium soy sauce, divided
1 (8-ounce) package presliced fresh mushrooms
1 medium turnip, chopped
1 small zucchini, sliced
1 small yellow squash, sliced
½ small eggplant, chopped
½ cup sliced celery
3 green onions, cut into 2-inch pieces
¼ teaspoon pepper
¼ teaspoon ground ginger
2 tablespoons dry sherry
1 tablespoon cornstarch
2½ cups cooked orzo (cooked without salt or fat)

Combine carrot, 2 tablespoons broth, and 1 tablespoon soy sauce in a nonstick skillet. Bring to a boil; cover, reduce heat, and cook 3 minutes. Add mushrooms and next 4 ingredients; cover and cook 7 minutes. Add celery, onions, pepper, and ginger; sauté 3 minutes.

   Combine remaining broth, remaining tablespoon soy sauce, sherry, and cornstarch. Add to skillet; cook over medium heat, stirring constantly, until thickened. Spoon over orzo.
Yield: 5 servings.

Per serving: Calories 173 (6% from fat)
Fat 1g (Sat tr   Mono tr   Poly tr)
Protein 7g   Carbohydrate 33g   Fiber 5g
Cholesterol 0mg   Sodium 429mg

FLORENTINE LASAGNA

Count 1 serving as:
3 Vegetable
1½ Starch
1 Meat/Dairy

♥ Good source of Folate, Calcium, and Potassium

9 lasagna noodles, uncooked
⅓ cup all-purpose flour
2¼ cups skim milk
1½ teaspoons dried basil
1 teaspoon salt
2 teaspoons olive oil
1 (8-ounce) package presliced fresh
    mushrooms
¼ cup dry white wine
3 cloves garlic, minced
1 small onion, chopped
2 (10-ounce) packages frozen chopped
    spinach, thawed and well drained
1 cup nonfat ricotta cheese
Vegetable cooking spray
4 medium carrots, shredded
1 cup (4 ounces) shredded part-skim
    mozzarella cheese
½ cup grated Parmesan cheese
¼ teaspoon paprika

Cook noodles according to package directions, omitting salt and fat. Drain; set aside.

Combine flour, milk, basil, and salt in a small bowl, stirring well with a wire whisk. Heat oil in a nonstick skillet over medium heat. Add mushrooms, wine, garlic, and onion; sauté until vegetables are tender.

Add flour mixture to mushroom mixture, and cook over medium heat, stirring constantly, until thickened. Remove from heat, and set aside.

Combine spinach and ricotta cheese in a small bowl, and set aside.

Place 3 lasagna noodles in a 13- x 9- x 2-inch baking dish coated with cooking spray. Spread half of spinach mixture over noodles. Sprinkle half of carrot over spinach. Sprinkle one-third of mozzarella cheese and one-third of Parmesan cheese over carrot, and top with one-third of mushroom mixture. Repeat layers. Top with remaining noodles, mushroom mixture, and cheeses.

Cover with aluminum foil coated with cooking spray, and bake at 300° for 1½ hours. Sprinkle with paprika, and let stand for 10 minutes before serving.
Yield: 8 servings.

Per serving: Calories 272 (20% from fat)
Fat 6g (Sat 2g   Mono 2g   Poly 1g)
Protein 19g   Carbohydrate 37g   Fiber 5g
Cholesterol 17mg   Sodium 572mg

Recipe pictured on page 20.

PASTA WITH ARTICHOKE-TOMATO SAUCE

Count 1 serving as:
2 Vegetable
1½ Starch

2 teaspoons olive oil
1 cup chopped onion
2 cloves garlic, minced
1 (15-ounce) can Italian-style chunky
    tomato sauce
½ teaspoon dried oregano
½ teaspoon dried basil
⅛ teaspoon sweet red pepper flakes
1 (16-ounce) can artichokes in water,
    drained and chopped
6 ounces whole wheat spinach noodles,
    uncooked
¼ cup freshly grated Parmesan cheese

Heat oil in a nonstick skillet over medium heat until hot. Add onion and garlic, and sauté until tender. Add tomato sauce and next 3 ingredients. Cover, reduce heat, and simmer 15 minutes. Add artichokes; cook 5 additional minutes.

   Cook pasta according to package directions, omitting salt and fat. Drain. To serve, spoon tomato sauce mixture over pasta, and top with Parmesan cheese.
Yield: 6 servings.

Per serving: Calories 172 (20% from fat)
Fat 4g (Sat 1g Mono 2g Poly 1g)
Protein 9g Carbohydrate 33g Fiber 6g
Cholesterol 28mg Sodium 426mg

EGGPLANT PARMESAN PASTA

Count 1 serving as:
3 Vegetable
1½ Starch
½ Meat/Dairy

♥ Good source of Vitamin C and Potassium

8 ounces spaghetti, uncooked
½ cup grated Parmesan cheese, divided
2 teaspoons olive oil
½ teaspoon garlic powder
¼ teaspoon salt
¼ teaspoon pepper
2 (1-pound) eggplants, peeled
Olive oil-flavored vegetable cooking spray
1 (26-ounce) jar meatless low-sodium,
    low-fat spaghetti sauce
1 cup (4 ounces) shredded part-skim
    mozzarella cheese

Cook pasta according to package directions, omitting salt and fat. Drain. Add ¼ cup Parmesan cheese, oil, and next 3 ingredients.

   Cut eggplants into ⅛-inch-thick slices; rinse with cold water, and pat dry. Coat with cooking spray. Coat a nonstick skillet with cooking spray; place over medium-high heat until hot. Cook eggplant 3 minutes on each side or until lightly browned. Cover, reduce heat, and cook 7 minutes or until tender.

   Place half of spaghetti mixture in a 13- x 9- x 2-inch baking dish coated with cooking spray. Add half of eggplant, half of spaghetti sauce, and ½ cup mozzarella cheese. Repeat layers. Top with remaining ¼ cup Parmesan cheese. Bake at 350° for 20 minutes.
Yield: 8 servings.

Per serving: Calories 254 (32% from fat)
Fat 7g (Sat 3g Mono 3g Poly 1g)
Protein 13g Carbohydrate 37g Fiber 5g
Cholesterol 13mg Sodium 561mg

PASTA PRIMAVERA

Count 1 serving as:
2 Vegetable
1½ Starch
½ Meat/Dairy
½ Fat

♥ Good source of Vitamin C, Folate, and Potassium

6 ounces small macaroni shells, uncooked
4 cups chopped broccoli
2 cups sliced yellow squash
2 cups sliced carrot
1 cup sliced sweet red pepper
½ cup sliced green onions
¾ teaspoon salt
¼ teaspoon black pepper
Dash of ground red pepper
3 cloves garlic, minced
⅔ cup water
½ cup low-fat sour cream
½ cup plain nonfat yogurt
¾ cup freshly grated Parmesan cheese, divided

Cook macaroni according to package directions, omitting salt and fat. Drain; set aside.

Combine broccoli and next 9 ingredients in a Dutch oven. Cook over medium heat, uncovered, 10 to 12 minutes or until vegetables are crisp-tender, stirring often. Add macaroni; cook until thoroughly heated. Remove from heat; stir in sour cream, yogurt, and ½ cup cheese. Transfer to a serving dish, and top with remaining ¼ cup cheese.
Yield: 6 (1½-cup) servings.

Per serving: Calories 241 (20% from fat)
Fat 5g (Sat 3g Mono 1g Poly 1g)
Protein 13g Carbohydrate 37g Fiber 5g
Cholesterol 15mg Sodium 546mg

ITALIAN SPAGHETTI SQUARES

Count 1 serving as:
2 Vegetable
1½ Starch
½ Meat/Dairy

8 ounces vermicelli, uncooked
¼ cup grated Parmesan cheese
¼ teaspoon garlic powder
½ cup fat-free egg substitute
Vegetable cooking spray
1 (15-ounce) can Italian-style tomato sauce
2 cups chopped fresh spinach
1 (8-ounce) package presliced fresh mushrooms
1 sweet yellow pepper, seeded and cut into strips
1 medium onion, sliced and separated into rings
4 plum tomatoes, sliced
1 cup (4 ounces) shredded part-skim mozzarella cheese

Cook pasta according to package directions, omitting salt and fat. Drain. Combine pasta, Parmesan cheese, and garlic powder in a large bowl. Add egg substitute, stirring well.

Spread pasta mixture evenly in a 13- x 9- x 2-inch baking dish coated with cooking spray. Press with back of spoon to form crust. Bake at 350° for 20 minutes. Spread tomato sauce on pasta crust. Top with spinach and remaining 5 ingredients. Bake at 375° for 25 minutes.
Yield: 8 servings.

Per serving: Calories 216 (18% from fat)
Fat 4g (Sat 2g Mono 1g Poly 1g)
Protein 12g Carbohydrate 33g Fiber 4g
Cholesterol 10mg Sodium 487mg

GARDEN PIZZA

Count 1 serving as:
2 Vegetable
1 Starch
½ Meat/Dairy

♥ Good source of Vitamin C and Potassium

1 (11-ounce) can refrigerated French bread dough
Olive oil-flavored vegetable cooking spray
2 cups chopped broccoli flowerets
1 cup sliced yellow squash
1 medium-size sweet red pepper, seeded and cut into strips
1 medium onion, sliced and separated into rings
1 clove garlic, minced
½ teaspoon dried basil
¼ teaspoon dried oregano
1 (8-ounce) can tomato sauce
¾ cup (3 ounces) shredded part-skim mozzarella cheese
¾ cup (3 ounces) shredded reduced-fat sharp Cheddar cheese

Press dough into a 15-inch pizza pan coated with cooking spray. Bake at 375° for 15 minutes. Remove from oven, and set aside.

Coat a large nonstick skillet with cooking spray; place over medium-high heat until hot. Add chopped broccoli, sliced yellow squash, sweet red pepper strips, onion rings, and minced garlic. Sauté 10 minutes or until vegetables are tender. Stir in dried basil and oregano, and set aside.

Spread tomato sauce on crust, and top with vegetable mixture. Sprinkle shredded mozzarella and shredded Cheddar evenly over vegetable mixture. Bake at 375° for 10 minutes or until cheese melts.
Yield: 8 servings.

Note: For a crispier crust, place pizza directly on oven rack for the second baking time.

Per serving: Calories 191 (24% from fat)
Fat 5g (Sat 3g   Mono 1g   Poly 1g)
Protein 11g   Carbohydrate 26g   Fiber 3g
Cholesterol 11mg   Sodium 532mg

Mushroom-Onion Pizza

Count 1 serving as:
2 Vegetable
1 Starch
½ Meat/Dairy

♥ Good source of
Potassium

1 (11-ounce) can refrigerated French bread
　dough
Vegetable cooking spray
1 pound fresh mushrooms, sliced
1 medium onion, sliced and separated into
　rings
1 clove garlic, minced
½ teaspoon dried basil
¼ teaspoon dried oregano
1 (8-ounce) can tomato sauce
1 cup (4 ounces) shredded part-skim
　mozzarella cheese
¼ cup freshly grated Parmesan cheese

Press dough into a 15-inch pizza pan coated
with cooking spray. Bake at 375° for 15 minutes. Remove from oven, and set aside.

　Coat a nonstick skillet with cooking spray,
and place over medium-high heat until hot.
Add mushrooms, onion, and garlic; sauté 7
minutes or until tender. Stir in dried basil and
oregano; set mixture aside.

　Spread tomato sauce on crust, and top with
vegetable mixture. Sprinkle cheeses evenly
over vegetable mixture. Bake at 375° for 10
minutes or until cheese melts.
Yield: 8 servings.

Per serving: Calories 188 (24% from fat)
Fat 5g (Sat 3g　Mono 1g　Poly 1g)
Protein 10g　Carbohydrate 26g　Fiber 3g
Cholesterol 10mg　Sodium 548mg

Veggie-Topped Baked Potatoes

Count 1 serving as:
1 Vegetable
1 Starch
½ Fat

♥ Good source of
Vitamin C and
Potassium

4 medium baking potatoes (about 1¾ pounds)
2 cups chopped broccoli
2 cups sliced yellow squash
¼ cup water
1 cup low-fat sour cream
¼ teaspoon salt
½ cup (2 ounces) shredded part-skim
　mozzarella cheese
2 tablespoons chopped fresh chives

Scrub potatoes; bake at 425° for 1 hour or
until tender.

　Combine broccoli, squash, and water in a
medium saucepan. Bring to a boil; cover,
reduce heat, and cook 5 minutes or until vegetables are crisp-tender. Drain and place in a
medium bowl. Add sour cream and salt; stir
well, and set aside.

　Cut baked potatoes in half lengthwise, and
fluff with a fork. Spoon vegetable mixture
evenly onto potato halves, and top evenly with
cheese and chives.
Yield: 8 servings (serving size: ½ potato with
topping).

Per serving: Calories 137 (22% from fat)
Fat 3g (Sat 2g　Mono 1g　Poly tr)
Protein 6g　Carbohydrate 22g　Fiber 3g
Cholesterol 14mg　Sodium 152mg

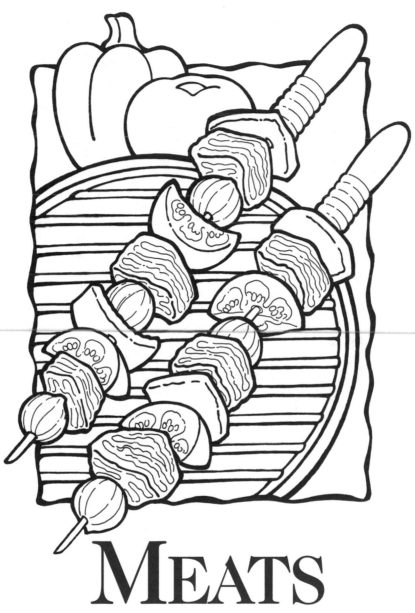

Meats

STUFFED GREEN PEPPERS

Count 1 serving as:
1 Vegetable
1 Starch
1 Meat/Dairy

♥ Good source of Vitamin C and Potassium

3 medium-size green peppers
½ pound ground round
½ cup chopped onion
1 (8-ounce) can tomato sauce
½ cup cooked bulgur wheat with soy grits
   (cooked without salt or fat)
2 teaspoons Worcestershire
   sauce
¼ teaspoon pepper
2 tablespoons (½ ounce) shredded
   reduced-fat sharp Cheddar cheese

Cut peppers in half lengthwise; remove and discard seeds and membranes. Place pepper halves in a large saucepan with water to cover; bring to a boil, and cook 5 minutes. Drain pepper halves, and set aside.

Combine meat and onion in a large non-stick skillet; cook over medium heat until meat is browned and onion is tender, stirring until meat crumbles. Add tomato sauce, cooked bulgur wheat, Worcestershire sauce, and ¼ teaspoon pepper; stir well.

Spoon meat mixture evenly into pepper halves. Place pepper halves in a 13- x 9- x 2-inch baking dish. Add hot water to baking dish to depth of ½ inch.

Bake, uncovered, at 350° for 25 minutes or until thoroughly heated. Top pepper halves evenly with shredded Cheddar cheese, and bake 5 additional minutes or until cheese melts. To serve, remove pepper halves from baking dish with a slotted spoon.
Yield: 3 servings (serving size: 2 pepper halves).

Note: If bulgur wheat with soy grits is not available, use regular bulgur.

Per serving: Calories 211 (23% from fat)
Fat 5g (Sat 2g   Mono 2g   Poly tr)
Protein 22g   Carbohydrate 21g   Fiber 4g
Cholesterol 48mg   Sodium 592mg

SAVORY MEAT LOAF

Count 1 serving as:
½ Starch
1 Meat/Dairy

½ pound ground round
½ pound freshly ground raw turkey
½ cup chopped onion
½ cup chopped green pepper
½ cup cooked bulgur wheat with soy grits (cooked without salt or fat)
¼ cup skim milk
2 tablespoons ketchup
1 tablespoon Worcestershire sauce
¼ teaspoon salt
¼ teaspoon pepper
¼ teaspoon ground thyme
¼ teaspoon dried marjoram
1 egg white, lightly beaten

Combine all ingredients in a large bowl; stir well. Spoon mixture into an 8½- x 4½- x 3-inch loafpan. Bake at 350° for 1 hour. Remove meat loaf from pan, and let cool slightly before slicing.
Yield: 6 servings.

Per serving: Calories 140 (19% from fat)
Fat 3g (Sat 1g Mono 1g Poly tr)
Protein 19g Carbohydrate 8g Fiber 1g
Cholesterol 45mg Sodium 235mg

MEATBALLS AND VEGETABLES

Count 1 serving as: ♥ Good source of
2 Vegetable   Vitamin C, Folate,
1½ Starch   and Potassium
1 Meat/Dairy

½ pound ground round
1 tablespoon dried parsley flakes
1 teaspoon soy sauce
¼ teaspoon garlic powder
Vegetable cooking spray
2 cups fresh broccoli flowerets
¾ cup thinly sliced carrot
6 green onions, sliced
1 (8-ounce) package presliced fresh mushrooms
1 cup canned ready to serve beef broth
1 tablespoon cornstarch
2 teaspoons soy sauce
¼ teaspoon salt
¼ teaspoon pepper
2 cups cooked yolk-free egg noodles (cooked without salt or fat)

Combine first 4 ingredients; shape into 12 balls. Place in a nonstick skillet coated with cooking spray. Cook over medium heat until browned on all sides. Add broccoli and next 3 ingredients. Cook, uncovered, 3 minutes or until meatballs are done. Remove from heat. Combine broth and next 4 ingredients; add to meatball mixture, and stir. Cook, uncovered, over medium heat until thickened. Serve over noodles.
Yield: 4 servings.

Per serving: Calories 287 (25% from fat)
Fat 8g (Sat 3g Mono 3g Poly 1g)
Protein 21g Carbohydrate 35g Fiber 6g
Cholesterol 34mg Sodium 642mg

Pork Tenderloin with
Mango Salsa (page 82)

BEEF AND BROCCOLI STIR-FRY

Count 1 serving as:
1 Vegetable
2 Starch
½ Meat/Dairy

♥ Good source of
Vitamin C, Folate,
and Potassium

¾ pound lean boneless round steak, well
    trimmed
1 cup water
¼ cup low-sodium soy sauce
3 tablespoons unsweetened apple juice
1 tablespoon cornstarch
1 teaspoon peeled, grated gingerroot
1 teaspoon beef-flavored bouillon granules
3 cloves garlic, minced
1 pound fresh broccoli
1 tablespoon vegetable oil
2 cups sliced onion
4 cups cooked brown rice (cooked without
    salt or fat)

Slice steak diagonally across grain into ¼-inch-thick strips. Place steak in a large heavy-duty, zip-top plastic bag. Combine water and next 6 ingredients, stirring well; pour over steak. Seal bag, and shake until steak is coated. Marinate in refrigerator 20 minutes, turning bag occasionally.

Trim broccoli; cut tops into flowerets, and cut stalks into ½-inch slices. Set aside.

Remove steak from marinade, reserving marinade. Heat oil in a Dutch oven over medium heat; add steak in batches, and cook until lightly browned. Remove steak from Dutch oven, and drain on paper towels. Set steak aside.

Add onion to Dutch oven, and sauté 1 minute. Stir in broccoli and ½ cup reserved marinade. Cover and cook 2 to 3 additional minutes or until broccoli is crisp-tender. Add steak and remaining marinade to broccoli mixture in Dutch oven; cook until mixture is slightly thickened, stirring occasionally. To serve, spoon steak mixture evenly over ½-cup portions of rice.
Yield: 8 servings.

Per serving: Calories 235 (16% from fat)
Fat 4g (Sat 1g   Mono 2g   Poly 1g)
Protein 15g   Carbohydrate 36g   Fiber 5g
Cholesterol 23mg   Sodium 505mg

SWISS-STYLE SIRLOIN

Count 1 serving as:
1 Meat/Dairy

1 teaspoon vegetable oil
1 pound cubed sirloin steak, cut into 6
    pieces
1 cup canned ready-to-serve beef broth
1 tablespoon cornstarch
2 tablespoons chopped onion
1 teaspoon diced pimiento
⅛ teaspoon salt

Heat vegetable oil in a large nonstick skillet over medium heat. Add steak, and cook until browned on both sides, turning once. Remove steak from skillet, and set aside.

Combine broth and cornstarch in a medium bowl, stirring well with a wire whisk. Add cornstarch mixture, onion, pimiento, and salt to skillet. Cook over medium heat, stirring constantly, until thickened. Return steak to skillet; cover, reduce heat, and simmer 45 minutes or until steak is tender.
Yield: 6 servings.

Per serving: Calories 103 (26% from fat)
Fat 3g (Sat 1g Mono 1g Poly tr)
Protein 16g Carbohydrate 2g Fiber tr
Cholesterol 40mg Sodium 189mg

BARBECUED ROUND STEAK

Count 1 serving as: ♥ Good source of
1½ Meat/Dairy   Potassium

⅓ cup cider vinegar
¼ cup ketchup
2 tablespoons Worcestershire sauce
1 teaspoon sugar
1 teaspoon dry mustard
1 teaspoon paprika
¼ teaspoon pepper
1 clove garlic, minced
1 pound lean boneless round steak, well
    trimmed

Combine first 8 ingredients in a small saucepan. Bring to a boil, reduce heat, and simmer, uncovered, 2 minutes.

Place steak in an 11- x 7- x 1½-inch baking dish. Add vinegar mixture. Cover and bake at 350° for 1 hour or until steak is tender. Serve steak with sauce.
Yield: 4 servings.

Per serving: Calories 161 (21% from fat)
Fat 4g (Sat 1g Mono 1g Poly tr)
Protein 23g Carbohydrate 8g Fiber tr
Cholesterol 60mg Sodium 296mg

Roast Beef Sandwiches

Count 1 serving as:
½ Vegetable
1 Starch
1 Meat/Dairy

♥ Good source of
  Potassium

2 tablespoons low-fat sour cream
2 tablespoons low-fat mayonnaise
½ teaspoon prepared horseradish
⅛ teaspoon dry mustard
4 (1-ounce) hard rolls
4 lettuce leaves
8 ounces thinly sliced cooked lean roast beef
    (cooked without salt)
1 medium tomato, cut into 4 slices

Combine first 4 ingredients in a small bowl,
stirring well.
  Cut each roll in half lengthwise, and spread
sour cream mixture evenly over roll halves.
Place lettuce leaves on 4 roll halves, and top
evenly with meat and tomato slices. Top with
remaining roll halves.
Yield: 4 servings.

Per serving: Calories 215 (21% from fat)
Fat 5g (Sat 2g Mono 2g Poly 1g)
Protein 22g Carbohydrate 20g Fiber 1g
Cholesterol 50mg Sodium 270mg

Marinated Filet Mignon

Count 1 serving as:
1½ Meat/Dairy

♥ Good source of
  Potassium

1 tablespoon Worcestershire sauce
1 tablespoon cider vinegar
1 teaspoon dried parsley flakes
½ teaspoon lemon-pepper seasoning
2 (4-ounce) beef tenderloin steaks, well
    trimmed
Vegetable cooking spray

Combine first 4 ingredients in a heavy-duty,
zip-top plastic bag. Add steaks to bag; seal bag,
and shake to coat steaks. Marinate in refrigerator 2 hours, turning bag occasionally.
  Remove steaks from marinade, reserving
marinade. Place marinade in a small saucepan; bring to a boil, and remove from heat.
Coat grill rack with cooking spray, and place
over hot coals (400° to 500°). Place steaks on
rack, and grill, uncovered, 7 minutes, basting
with reserved marinade. Turn steaks, and
cook 5 to 7 minutes or to desired degree of
doneness.
Yield: 2 servings.

Per serving: Calories 159 (39% from fat)
Fat 7g (Sat 3g Mono 3g Poly tr)
Protein 21g Carbohydrate 2g Fiber tr
Cholesterol 56mg Sodium 210mg

Veal Tetrazzini

6 ounces spaghetti, uncooked
Butter-flavored vegetable cooking spray
1 (16-ounce) package presliced fresh
   mushrooms
1 pound veal, cut into strips
1 clove garlic, minced
¼ cup dry white wine, divided
⅛ teaspoon ground nutmeg
1 (14¼-ounce) can ready-to-serve chicken
   broth
2 tablespoons flour
½ teaspoon pepper
¼ teaspoon salt
½ cup evaporated skimmed milk
¼ cup skim milk
⅓ cup grated Parmesan cheese

Break spaghetti into 2-inch pieces. Cook according to package directions, omitting salt and fat; drain and set aside.

Coat a medium nonstick skillet with cooking spray; place over medium-high heat until hot. Add mushrooms, and sauté 3 to 5 minutes or until tender. Remove mushrooms from skillet, and set aside. Add veal and garlic to skillet; cook over medium heat until veal is browned on all sides. Add mushrooms, 2 tablespoons wine, and nutmeg to skillet; cook over medium-high heat until thoroughly heated. Remove from heat, and set aside.

Combine broth, flour, pepper, and salt in a small saucepan, stirring well with a wire whisk. Bring to a boil, and cook, stirring constantly, 2 minutes. Remove from heat, and stir in evaporated milk, skim milk, and remaining 2 tablespoons wine.

Place spaghetti in a 13- x 9- x 2-inch baking dish coated with cooking spray. Pour half of broth mixture over spaghetti. Top with veal mixture. Pour remaining broth mixture over veal mixture. Sprinkle evenly with cheese. Bake at 400° for 20 minutes or until lightly browned and bubbly.
Yield: 6 servings.

Per serving: Calories 272 (17% from fat)
Fat 5g (Sat 2g   Mono 2g   Poly 1g)
Protein 22g   Carbohydrate 32g   Fiber 2g
Cholesterol 52mg   Sodium 471mg

CURRIED LAMB

Count 1 serving as:
1 Fruit
1½ Starch
1 Meat/Dairy

♥ Good source of
Potassium

1 pound lean boneless lamb
1 cup water
½ teaspoon salt
2 cloves garlic, minced
4 cups diced cooking apple
1 cup diced celery
1 cup sliced onion
1 teaspoon curry powder
3 cups cooked brown rice (cooked without
    salt or fat)

Trim fat from lamb; cut lamb into 1-inch cubes. Place lamb, water, salt, and garlic in a large saucepan, and bring to a boil over medium-high heat. Cover, reduce heat, and cook 30 minutes or until lamb is tender.

   Add apple, celery, onion, and curry powder to lamb mixture, stirring well. Cover and cook 15 minutes. To serve, spoon lamb mixture evenly over ½-cup portions of rice.
Yield: 6 servings.

Per serving: Calories 285 (21% from fat)
Fat 7g (Sat 2g   Mono 3g   Poly 1g)
Protein 20g   Carbohydrate 36g   Fiber 5g
Cholesterol 54mg   Sodium 259mg

RED BEANS WITH HAM

Count 1 serving as:
2 Starch

♥ Good source of
Folate and Potassium

1 cup dried red kidney beans
3½ cups water
½ cup chopped onion
½ cup chopped green pepper
¼ cup (1 ounce) chopped lean ham
¼ teaspoon garlic salt
¼ teaspoon ground savory
⅛ teaspoon ground thyme
⅛ teaspoon pepper

Sort and rinse beans. Place beans, water, and remaining ingredients in a Dutch oven, and bring to a boil. Cover, reduce heat, and simmer 2½ hours or until beans are tender and liquid is thickened.
Yield: 4 (¾-cup) servings.

Per serving: Calories 168 (6% from fat)
Fat 1g (Sat tr   Mono tr   Poly tr)
Protein 12g   Carbohydrate 29g   Fiber 8g
Cholesterol 4mg   Sodium 166mg

SWEET-AND-SOUR PORK

Count 1 serving as:
1 Vegetable
1 Fruit
1 Starch
1 Meat/Dairy

♥ Good source of
Vitamin C and
Potassium

1 (8-ounce) can pineapple chunks in juice,
    undrained
3 tablespoons low-sodium soy sauce, divided
1 pound lean boneless pork loin, thinly
    sliced
Vegetable cooking spray
1 cup thinly sliced carrot
1 tablespoon water
1 medium-size green pepper, seeded and
    cut into ½-inch strips
1 medium onion, cut into 6 wedges and
    separated
1 cup water
¼ cup red wine vinegar
2 tablespoons cornstarch
1 tablespoon sugar
3 cups cooked brown rice (cooked without
    salt or fat)

Drain pineapple, reserving juice; set pineapple aside. Combine pineapple juice and 1 tablespoon soy sauce. Place pork in a shallow dish; pour pineapple juice mixture over pork, turning to coat pork. Cover and marinate in refrigerator 1 hour.

Remove pork from marinade, discarding marinade. Coat a nonstick skillet with cooking spray; place over medium-high heat until hot. Add pork; stir-fry until browned. Set pork aside, and keep warm.

Add carrot and 1 tablespoon water to skillet; cover and cook 2 minutes. Stir in green pepper and onion. Stir-fry 4 minutes. Add 1 tablespoon soy sauce and reserved pineapple; stir-fry 1 minute.

Combine remaining 1 tablespoon soy sauce, 1 cup water, vinegar, cornstarch, and sugar in a small bowl, stirring well with a wire whisk. Add vinegar mixture to vegetable mixture, and cook, stirring constantly, until thickened and bubbly. Stir in pork. To serve, spoon pork mixture evenly over ½-cup portions of rice.
Yield: 6 servings.

Per serving: Calories 278 (13% from fat)
Fat 4g (Sat 1g Mono 2g Poly 1g)
Protein 21g Carbohydrate 40g Fiber 4g
Cholesterol 48mg Sodium 348mg

PORK TENDERLOIN WITH MANGO SALSA

Count 1 serving as:
1½ Fruit
1½ Meat/Dairy

♥ Good source of Vitamin C and Potassium

2 (¾-pound) pork tenderloins
1 tablespoon soy sauce
Vegetable cooking spray
3 ripe mangoes, peeled and chopped
¼ cup raisins
¼ cup chopped purple onion
1 tablespoon lemon juice

Brush pork with soy sauce. Coat grill rack with cooking spray; place rack on grill over medium-hot coals (350° to 400°). Place pork on rack; grill, covered, 15 to 20 minutes or until a meat thermometer inserted into thickest part of one tenderloin registers 160°, turning once. Let pork stand 10 minutes before slicing.

Combine mango and remaining 3 ingredients in a medium saucepan. Cook over medium heat until thoroughly heated, stirring occasionally. To serve, top pork slices evenly with mango salsa.
Yield: 6 servings.

Baking instructions: Place pork in an 11- x 7- x 1½-inch baking dish coated with cooking spray. Bake at 325° for 50 minutes or until meat thermometer registers 160°.

Per serving: Calories 240 (18% from fat)
Fat 5g (Sat 2g   Mono 2g   Poly tr)
Protein 27g   Carbohydrate 24g   Fiber 2g
Cholesterol 72mg   Sodium 226mg

Recipe pictured on page 74.

ROASTED PORK LOIN

Count 1 serving as:
1 Vegetable
2 Starch
1 Meat/Dairy
½ Fat

♥ Good source of Potassium

1 (1½-pound) lean boneless center-cut pork loin roast
2 teaspoons pepper
1 teaspoon salt
3 cloves garlic, thinly sliced
1 tablespoon olive oil
2 pounds small round red potatoes
4 medium onions, peeled and halved
1 (8-ounce) package baby carrots
1 cup water
1 cup dry white wine
1 tablespoon cornstarch

Trim fat from roast; sprinkle roast with pepper and salt. Cut small slits in top of roast; place a garlic slice in each slit. Heat oil in an oven-proof Dutch oven over medium heat. Add roast; cook until browned on all sides.

Add potatoes and next 4 ingredients to Dutch oven. Cover and bake at 350° for 1 hour or until meat and vegetables are tender.

Transfer roast and vegetables to a serving platter. Add cornstarch to liquid in Dutch oven, and stir with a wire whisk. Bring to a boil, and cook, stirring constantly, 1 minute. Spoon sauce over roast and vegetables.
Yield: 8 servings.

Per serving: Calories 323 (24% from fat)
Fat 9g (Sat 3g   Mono 4g   Poly 1g)
Protein 22g   Carbohydrate 34g   Fiber 4g
Cholesterol 55mg   Sodium 344mg

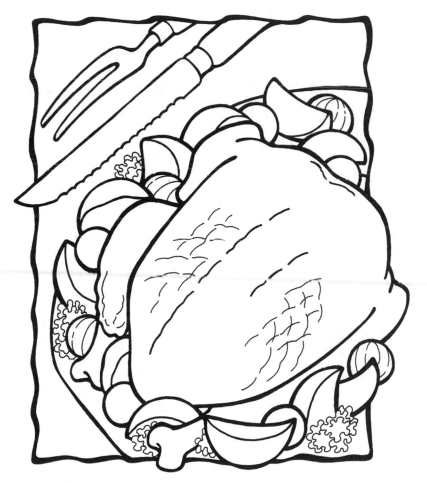

POULTRY

ALMOND-CHICKEN CRÊPES

Count 1 serving as:
½ Fruit
1 Starch
1 Meat/Dairy

♥ Good source of
Potassium

1 cup canned ready-to-serve chicken broth
1 tablespoon cornstarch
¼ teaspoon salt
2 cups chopped cooked chicken breast
(skinned before cooking and cooked
without salt)
1 (11-ounce) can mandarin oranges in light
syrup, drained
1 (8-ounce) can sliced water chestnuts,
drained and coarsely chopped
¼ cup chopped green onions
2 tablespoons dry white wine
16 Crêpes
1½ cups plain nonfat yogurt
2 tablespoons dry white wine
2 tablespoons sliced almonds

Combine broth, cornstarch, and salt in a
saucepan. Cook over medium heat, stirring
constantly, until thickened. Remove from
heat. Stir in chicken and next 4 ingredients.

Spoon ¼ cup chicken mixture down center
of each crêpe. Roll up each crêpe, and place,
seam side down, in a 13- x 9- x 2-inch baking
dish. Combine yogurt and 2 tablespoons wine
in a small bowl, stirring well with a wire
whisk. Spread yogurt mixture over crêpes.
Sprinkle with almonds. Bake at 375° for 10
minutes or until crêpes are thoroughly heated.
Yield: 8 servings (serving size: 2 crêpes).

CRÊPES

1 cup fat-free egg substitute
1 cup skim milk
¼ teaspoon salt
1¼ cups all-purpose flour
Vegetable cooking spray

Combine egg substitute, milk, and salt in a
medium bowl. Beat at medium speed of an
electric mixer for 1 minute. Add flour, and
beat until smooth. Cover and chill at least
20 minutes.

Coat bottom of an 8-inch nonstick skillet
with cooking spray; place over medium heat
until hot. Pour about 3 tablespoons batter into
skillet; quickly tilt skillet in all directions so
batter covers bottom of skillet. Cook 1 minute
or until crêpe can be shaken loose from skillet.
Turn crêpe, and cook about 30 seconds. Place
crêpe on a dish towel to cool. Repeat proce-
dure with remaining batter. (Do not stack
crêpes.)
Yield: 16 crêpes.

Per serving: Calories 228 (10% from fat)
Fat 3g (Sat 1g Mono 1g Poly 1g)
Protein 19g Carbohydrate 30g Fiber 2g
Cholesterol 27mg Sodium 353mg

CHICKEN QUICHE

Count 1 serving as:
1 Vegetable
1 Meat/Dairy

♥ Good source of Calcium and Potassium

1 cup chopped cooked chicken breast
   (skinned before cooking and cooked
   without salt)
1 (10-ounce) package frozen chopped
   broccoli, thawed
Butter-flavored vegetable cooking spray
1 cup nonfat ricotta cheese
½ cup plain nonfat yogurt
½ cup fat-free egg substitute
⅓ cup grated Parmesan cheese
¼ cup whole wheat flour
½ teaspoon baking powder
½ teaspoon dry mustard
¼ teaspoon salt
⅛ teaspoon ground red pepper

Combine chicken and broccoli; place in a
9-inch pieplate coated with cooking spray.
   Combine ricotta cheese and remaining 8
ingredients in container of an electric blender.
Cover and process until smooth, stopping
once to scrape down sides. Pour cheese mixture over chicken mixture in pieplate. Bake at
350° for 40 to 45 minutes or until a knife inserted in center comes out clean. Let stand 10
minutes before slicing into wedges.
Yield: 6 servings.

Per serving: Calories 148 (19% from fat)
Fat 3g (Sat 2g   Mono 1g   Poly 0g)
Protein 19g   Carbohydrate 11g   Fiber 2g
Cholesterol 23mg   Sodium 348mg

CURRIED CHICKEN SALAD

Count 1 serving as:
½ Fruit
1 Meat/Dairy

½ cup low-fat mayonnaise
½ teaspoon curry powder
2 cups chopped cooked chicken breast
   (skinned before cooking and cooked
   without salt)
½ cup raisins
½ cup chopped celery
2 tablespoons sliced green onions

Combine mayonnaise and curry powder in a
medium bowl, stirring well. Add chicken and
remaining ingredients, stirring to combine.
Cover and chill at least 1 hour.
Yield: 6 (½-cup) servings.

Per serving: Calories 147 (19% from fat)
Fat 3g (Sat 1g   Mono 1g   Poly 1g)
Protein 14g   Carbohydrate 16g   Fiber 1g
Cholesterol 35mg   Sodium 227mg

Chicken Kabobs

Count 1 serving as:
½ Vegetable
2 Starch
1 Meat/Dairy

♥ Good source of
Potassium

1 tablespoon peanut butter
2 tablespoons low-sodium soy sauce
¼ teaspoon hot sauce
⅛ teaspoon ground ginger
1 pound skinned, boned chicken breasts, cut
    into 1-inch pieces
12 medium-size fresh mushrooms
6 green onions, cut into 2-inch pieces
12 cherry tomatoes
Vegetable cooking spray
3 cups Yellow and Brown Rice (page 53)

Combine first 4 ingredients; stir well. Place
chicken in a large heavy-duty, zip-top plastic
bag; add peanut butter mixture. Seal bag, and
shake until chicken is well coated. Marinate in
refrigerator 30 minutes, turning once.

    Remove chicken from marinade, reserving
marinade. Place marinade in a saucepan;
bring to a boil. Remove from heat; set aside.

    Alternately thread chicken, mushrooms,
green onions, and tomatoes on 6 (10-inch)
metal skewers. Place kabobs on rack of a
broiler pan coated with cooking spray. Baste
with marinade. Broil 8 minutes. Turn and
broil 5 additional minutes or until chicken is
tender. Serve over Yellow and Brown Rice.
Yield: 6 servings.

Per serving: Calories 281 (16% from fat)
Fat 5g (Sat 1g Mono 2g Poly 1g)
Protein 22g Carbohydrate 38g Fiber 3g
Cholesterol 41mg Sodium 469mg

Chicken Salad Stuffed Tomatoes

Count 1 serving as:
1½ Vegetable
1 Meat/Dairy
½ Fat

♥ Good source of
Vitamin C and
Potassium

1 pound skinned, boned chicken breasts
1 stalk celery
½ medium carrot
1 cup chopped celery
⅓ cup low-fat mayonnaise
1 tablespoon lemon juice
½ teaspoon salt
¼ teaspoon salt-free lemon-herb seasoning
6 medium tomatoes
6 lettuce leaves
¼ cup sliced almonds, toasted

Place first 3 ingredients in a Dutch oven; add
water to cover. Bring to a boil; cover, reduce
heat, and simmer 30 minutes or until chicken
is tender. Let chicken cool slightly.

    Remove chicken from broth, and cut into
bite-size pieces. (Reserve broth, celery stalk,
and carrot half for another use.) Combine
chicken, chopped celery, and next 4 ingredients. Cover and chill.

    Cut an "X" in the top of each tomato, cutting
to but not through bottoms. Pull tomatoes
open; top evenly with chicken mixture. Place
tomatoes on lettuce leaves; top with almonds.
Yield: 6 servings.

Per serving: Calories 166 (31% from fat)
Fat 6g (Sat 1g Mono 3g Poly 2g)
Protein 19g Carbohydrate 11g Fiber 2g
Cholesterol 41mg Sodium 384mg

MEXICAN CHICKEN ON POLENTA

Count 1 serving as:
2 Starch
1 Meat/Dairy

♥ Good source of
Potassium

2 cups water
¼ teaspoon salt
¾ cup stone-ground cornmeal
Butter-flavored vegetable cooking spray
1 pound skinned, boned chicken breasts, cut
    into bite-size pieces
¼ cup chopped sweet red pepper
¼ cup chopped green onions
1 tablespoon lime juice
1 teaspoon minced canned jalapeño pepper
¾ teaspoon chili powder
½ teaspoon ground cumin
¼ teaspoon salt
1 clove garlic, minced
½ cup low-fat sour cream

Combine water and ¼ teaspoon salt in a medium saucepan; bring to a boil. Add cornmeal in a slow, steady stream, stirring constantly. Reduce heat to medium, and cook, stirring constantly, 10 minutes or until mixture pulls away from sides of pan.

Place a 9-inch square pan in a 450° oven for 1 minute. Remove from oven, and coat with cooking spray. Spoon cornmeal mixture (polenta) into pan, and spread with a spatula coated with cooking spray. Lightly coat surface of polenta with cooking spray. Broil 3 inches from heat (with electric oven door partially opened) 3 to 5 minutes or until lightly browned. Cut into 4 triangles. Set aside, and keep warm.

Coat a large nonstick skillet with cooking spray; place over medium-high heat until hot. Add chicken and next 8 ingredients; stir-fry 8 minutes or until chicken is tender. Remove from heat, and stir in sour cream. To serve, spoon chicken mixture over polenta triangles. **Yield:** 4 servings.

Per serving: Calories 279 (19% from fat)
Fat 6g (Sat 2g   Mono 2g   Poly 1g)
Protein 29g   Carbohydrate 27g   Fiber 3g
Cholesterol 72mg   Sodium 395mg

CASHEW CHICKEN

Count 1 serving as:
½ Vegetable
½ Fruit
2 Starch
1 Meat/Dairy

♥ Good source of
Vitamin C and
Potassium

1 pound skinned, boned chicken breasts, cut
    into strips
¼ cup unsweetened orange juice
1 tablespoon plus 1 teaspoon cornstarch,
    divided
1 teaspoon sesame oil
¼ cup chopped cashews
1 (8-ounce) can sliced water chestnuts,
    drained
1 cup chopped green pepper
½ cup chopped green onions
1 tablespoon peeled, minced gingerroot
1 cup canned ready-to-serve chicken broth
2 tablespoons low-sodium soy sauce
1 (11-ounce) can mandarin oranges in light
    syrup, drained
3 cups cooked brown rice (cooked without
    salt or fat)

Combine chicken, orange juice, and 1 tea-spoon cornstarch in a medium bowl; cover and chill 1 hour.

Heat oil in a nonstick skillet over medium heat. Add cashews, and stir-fry 30 seconds. Remove from skillet, and set cashews aside.

Add chicken mixture to skillet. Cook, uncovered, over medium-high heat 8 minutes or until liquid evaporates and chicken is lightly browned. Add water chestnuts and next 3 ingredients; stir-fry 5 minutes or until pepper is crisp-tender. Remove from heat.

Combine chicken broth, soy sauce, and re-maining 1 tablespoon cornstarch; add to chicken mixture. Bring to a boil; reduce heat to medium, and cook, stirring constantly, until thickened. Cook 1 additional minute. Remove from heat, and stir in orange sec-tions. To serve, spoon chicken mixture over rice, and sprinkle with cashews.
Yield: 6 servings (serving size: ¾ cup chicken mixture and ½ cup rice).

Per serving: Calories 308 (20% from fat)
Fat 7g (Sat 2g   Mono 3g   Poly 2g)
Protein 22g   Carbohydrate 40g   Fiber 3g
Cholesterol 41mg   Sodium 414mg

Recipe pictured on page 92.

CHICKEN AND RICE CASSEROLE

Count 1 serving as:
1 Starch
1 Meat/Dairy

♥ Good source of Potassium

1 pound skinned, boned chicken breasts
1 bay leaf
Butter-flavored vegetable cooking spray
¼ cup chopped onion
¼ cup chopped celery
¼ cup all-purpose flour
¾ cup evaporated skimmed milk
1 teaspoon chicken-flavored bouillon granules
2 cups cooked brown rice (cooked without salt or fat)
¼ cup freshly grated Parmesan cheese
¼ teaspoon salt
¼ teaspoon black pepper
Dash of ground red pepper
¼ teaspoon paprika

Place chicken and bay leaf in a Dutch oven; add water to cover. Bring to a boil; cover, reduce heat, and simmer 20 minutes or until chicken is tender. Drain chicken, reserving 1½ cups broth. Remove and discard bay leaf. Let chicken cool slightly, and cut into bite-size pieces; set aside.

Coat a medium saucepan with cooking spray; add 2 tablespoons reserved broth, and place over medium-high heat until hot. Add onion and celery, and sauté until tender. Add flour, and stir with a wire whisk until smooth. Gradually add remaining broth, milk, and bouillon granules; cook over medium heat, stirring constantly, until slightly thickened. Stir in chicken, rice, and next 4 ingredients.

Spoon mixture into a 2-quart baking dish coated with cooking spray. Sprinkle with paprika. Bake at 350° for 25 minutes or until thoroughly heated.
Yield: 8 (1-cup) servings.

Per serving: Calories 173 (16% from fat)
Fat 3g (Sat 1g   Mono 1g   Poly 1g)
Protein 17g   Carbohydrate 18g   Fiber 1g
Cholesterol 34mg   Sodium 352mg

SKILLET RICE AND CHICKEN

<table>
<tr><td>Count 1 serving as:
1 Vegetable
1½ Starch
1 Meat/Dairy</td><td>♥ Good source of
Vitamin C, Folate,
and Potassium</td></tr>
</table>

1 pound fresh asparagus
1 pound skinned, boned chicken breast
  halves
2 tablespoons lemon juice
1 tablespoon olive oil
2 cloves garlic, minced
½ cup chopped onion
¼ cup chopped lean ham
2 tablespoons sliced green olives
½ teaspoon salt
1 cup brown rice, uncooked
2 medium tomatoes, coarsely chopped
1 (14¼-ounce) can ready-to-serve chicken
  broth
1 (10-ounce) package frozen English peas,
  thawed

Snap off tough ends of asparagus. Remove scales with a knife or vegetable peeler, if desired. Set aside.

Cut each chicken breast half into 4 strips, and drizzle evenly with lemon juice.

Heat oil in a large nonstick skillet over medium-high heat. Add chicken and garlic; cook, uncovered, until chicken is browned on all sides, stirring often. Add onion, ham, olives, and salt. Cook, stirring constantly, until onion is tender.

Spread rice over chicken mixture in skillet. Top with tomato. Add chicken broth (do not stir). Bring to a boil; cover, reduce heat, and cook 55 minutes.

Spread peas evenly over rice. Top with asparagus spears. Cover and cook 15 minutes or until asparagus is tender.
Yield: 8 servings.

Per serving: Calories 234 (20% from fat)
Fat 5g (Sat 1g   Mono 2g   Poly 1g)
Protein 20g   Carbohydrate 28g   Fiber 5g
Cholesterol 33mg   Sodium 475mg

CHICKEN PASTA PRIMAVERA

Count 1 serving as:
1 Vegetable
1 Starch
1 Meat/Dairy

♥ Good source of
Potassium

---

8 ounces fettuccini, uncooked
Olive oil-flavored vegetable cooking spray
1 pound skinned, boned chicken breasts, cut
    into strips
1 clove garlic, minced
1 (10-ounce) package frozen snow pea pods
½ cup evaporated skimmed milk
¼ teaspoon salt
¼ teaspoon pepper
½ cup freshly grated Parmesan cheese

Cook pasta according to package directions,
omitting salt and fat. Drain; place in a bowl.
    Coat a nonstick skillet with cooking spray;
place over medium heat until hot. Add chicken
and garlic; sauté until chicken is lightly
browned. Add chicken to pasta, and set aside.
    Add peas to skillet; sauté 3 minutes. Add to
pasta mixture; toss. Place in a 13- x 9- x 2-
inch baking dish coated with cooking spray.
    Add milk, salt, and pepper to skillet, stirring
to combine. Cook over medium heat until
thoroughly heated (do not boil). Pour milk
mixture over pasta mixture (do not stir). Top
with Parmesan cheese, and bake at 350° for
20 minutes or until thoroughly heated.
Yield: 8 servings.

Per serving: Calories 221 (19% from fat)
Fat 5g (Sat 2g   Mono 1g   Poly 1g)
Protein 21g   Carbohydrate 23g   Fiber 2g
Cholesterol 61mg   Sodium 242mg

*Cashew Chicken
(page 88)*

BARBECUED CHICKEN

Count 1 serving as:
½ Starch
1 Meat/Dairy

♥ Good source of
Potassium

---

1 tablespoon brown sugar
3 tablespoons ketchup
2 tablespoons water
1 teaspoon chili powder
2 teaspoons cider vinegar
1 teaspoon Worcestershire sauce
½ teaspoon paprika
4 (4-ounce) skinned, boned chicken
    breast halves

Combine first 7 ingredients in a small bowl.
Place chicken in a 1-quart baking dish. Pour
ketchup mixture over chicken; turn chicken
to coat all sides. Cover and bake at 350° for 35
to 40 minutes or until chicken is tender.
Yield: 4 servings.

Per serving: Calories 161 (18% from fat)
Fat 3g (Sat 1g   Mono 1g   Poly 1g)
Protein 25g   Carbohydrate 7g   Fiber tr
Cholesterol 62mg   Sodium 211mg

HAWAIIAN CHICKEN

Count 1 serving as:
½ Fruit
1 Starch
1 Meat/Dairy

♥ Good source of
Potassium

1 (8-ounce) can crushed pineapple in juice,
  undrained
¼ cup unsweetened orange juice
¼ cup dark corn syrup
1 teaspoon soy sauce
½ teaspoon cornstarch
¼ teaspoon ground ginger
¼ teaspoon pepper
⅛ teaspoon salt
4 (4-ounce) skinned, boned chicken breast
  halves

Combine first 8 ingredients in a saucepan.
Cook over medium heat, stirring constantly,
until thickened. Remove mixture from heat.
   Place chicken in a 13- x 9- x 2-inch baking
dish. Spoon pineapple mixture over chicken.
Bake, uncovered, at 375° for 25 to 30 minutes
or until chicken is tender.
Yield: 4 servings.

Per serving: Calories 235 (12% from fat)
Fat 3g (Sat 1g   Mono 1g   Poly 1g)
Protein 25g   Carbohydrate 27g   Fiber 1g
Cholesterol 62mg   Sodium 238mg

LEMON-PEPPER CHICKEN

Count 1 serving as:
½ Starch
1½ Meat/Dairy

♥ Good source of
Potassium

4 (4-ounce) skinned, boned chicken breast
  halves
¼ cup plain nonfat yogurt
½ cup fine, dry breadcrumbs
½ teaspoon paprika
½ teaspoon lemon-pepper seasoning
Vegetable cooking spray

Coat chicken with yogurt. Combine breadcrumbs, paprika, and lemon-pepper seasoning
in a shallow bowl. Dredge chicken in breadcrumb mixture.
   Place chicken in an 11- x 7- x 1½-inch
baking dish coated with cooking spray. Bake,
uncovered, at 425° for 15 minutes or until
chicken is tender.
Yield: 4 servings.

Per serving: Calories 196 (18% from fat)
Fat 4g (Sat 1g   Mono 1g   Poly 1g)
Protein 27g   Carbohydrate 11g   Fiber tr
Cholesterol 62mg   Sodium 228mg

Raspberry Chicken with Brown Rice

Count 1 serving as:
1 Fruit
2 Starch
1 Meat/Dairy

♥ Good source of
Potassium

Vegetable cooking spray
4 (4-ounce) skinned, boned chicken breast
   halves
¼ teaspoon salt
½ cup no-sugar-added raspberry fruit spread
¼ cup unsweetened orange juice
1 teaspoon prepared horseradish
2 cups cooked brown rice (cooked without
   salt or fat)

Coat a large nonstick skillet with cooking
spray; place over medium heat until hot. Add
chicken, and sprinkle evenly with salt. Cook
over medium heat 12 minutes or until
chicken is tender, turning to brown both
sides. Remove chicken from skillet; set aside,
and keep warm.

Add fruit spread, orange juice, and horseradish to skillet. Bring to a boil over medium-
high heat, and cook, stirring constantly, 1
minute. To serve, place chicken breast halves
on ½ cup portions of rice, and top evenly with
raspberry mixture.
Yield: 4 servings.

Per serving: Calories 343 (11% from fat)
Fat 4g (Sat 1g   Mono 1g   Poly 1g)
Protein 28g   Carbohydrate 48g   Fiber 4g
Cholesterol 62mg   Sodium 211mg

Rosemary-Ginger Chicken

Count 1 serving as:
1 Meat/Dairy

4 (4-ounce) skinned, boned chicken breast
   halves
Butter-flavored vegetable cooking spray
2 tablespoons lemon juice
1 teaspoon ground ginger
1 teaspoon minced fresh rosemary
¼ teaspoon salt

Place chicken on a baking sheet coated with
cooking spray. Drizzle lemon juice evenly over
chicken; sprinkle with ginger, rosemary, and
salt. Bake, uncovered, at 350° for 20 minutes
or until tender.
Yield: 4 servings.

Per serving: Calories 136 (21% from fat)
Fat 3g (Sat 1g   Mono 1g   Poly 1g)
Protein 25g   Carbohydrate 1g   Fiber tr
Cholesterol 62mg   Sodium 204mg

CHICKEN SUPREME

Count 1 serving as:
1 Vegetable
½ Starch
1 Meat/Dairy

♥ Good source of
  Potassium

---

4 (4-ounce) skinned, boned chicken breast
  halves
Butter-flavored vegetable cooking spray
1 (8-ounce) package presliced fresh
  mushrooms
¼ cup sliced green onions
½ cup skim milk
¼ cup canned ready-to-serve chicken broth
2 tablespoons dry white wine
2 tablespoons all-purpose flour
⅛ teaspoon salt
¼ teaspoon pepper

Place chicken in a nonstick skillet coated with
cooking spray. Cook over medium heat until
browned, turning once. Remove from skillet;
set aside.

Add mushrooms and onions to skillet; sauté
until tender. Transfer to an 11- x 7- x 1½-inch
baking dish. Place chicken over vegetables.
Cover and bake at 400° for 15 minutes or
until chicken is tender.

Combine milk, broth, and wine; set aside.
Add flour to skillet. Cook flour over medium
heat, stirring constantly, 2 minutes. Gradually
add broth mixture, salt, and pepper, stirring
well with a wire whisk. Cook over medium-
high heat, stirring constantly, until thickened.
To serve, pour sauce over chicken.
Yield: 4 servings.

Per serving: Calories 180 (17% from fat)
Fat 4g (Sat 1g   Mono 1g   Poly 1g)
Protein 27g   Carbohydrate 8g   Fiber 1g
Cholesterol 63mg   Sodium 194mg

TANGY TURKEY SPAGHETTI

Count 1 serving as:
2 Vegetable
2½ Starch
½ Meat/Dairy

♥ Good source of
  Vitamin C and
  Potassium

Vegetable cooking spray
1 teaspoon olive oil
½ pound freshly ground raw turkey
2 tablespoons minced onion
2 teaspoons seeded and minced fresh
  jalapeño pepper
2 cloves garlic, crushed
1 (14½-ounce) can diced tomatoes,
  undrained
½ cup water
⅓ cup tomato paste
2 tablespoons balsamic vinegar
1 tablespoon plus 1 teaspoon lemon juice
¼ teaspoon dried oregano
4 cups cooked spaghetti (cooked without
  salt or fat)

Coat a large nonstick skillet with cooking
spray; add oil, and place over medium heat
until hot. Add turkey and next 3 ingredients;
cook until turkey is browned, stirring until it
crumbles.

Add tomatoes and next 5 ingredients to
turkey mixture. Cover, reduce heat, and simmer 25 minutes, stirring occasionally. To
serve, spoon ½ cup sauce over 1 cup spaghetti.
Yield: 4 servings.

Per serving: Calories 327 (12% from fat)
Fat 4g (Sat 1g   Mono 1g   Poly 1g)
Protein 22g   Carbohydrate 50g   Fiber 4g
Cholesterol 34mg   Sodium 394mg

TURKEY-CHILI PIE

Count 1 serving as:
2 Starch
1 Meat/Dairy

♥ Good source of
Calcium and
Potassium

Rice Crust
8 ounces freshly ground raw turkey
½ cup chopped onion
Vegetable cooking spray
1 (10-ounce) package frozen whole-kernel
    corn
1 tablespoon canned chopped jalapeño
    pepper
2 teaspoons chili powder
½ teaspoon cumin seeds
1 cup (4 ounces) shredded reduced-fat sharp
    Cheddar cheese
½ cup fat-free egg substitute
1 cup evaporated skimmed milk
¼ teaspoon salt
¼ teaspoon pepper

Prepare Rice Crust, and set aside.

Place turkey and onion in a large skillet
coated with cooking spray. Cook over medium
heat until turkey is browned, stirring until it
crumbles.

Add corn to skillet; cover and cook 3 minutes. Remove skillet from heat, and add
chopped jalapeño pepper, chili powder, and
cumin seeds. Spoon turkey mixture into Rice
Crust. Top with shredded Cheddar cheese, and
set aside.

Combine egg substitute, milk, salt, and
¼ teaspoon pepper in a medium bowl, stirring
well with a wire whisk. Pour egg substitute
mixture over turkey mixture. Bake at 350° for
30 minutes or until set.
Yield: 8 servings.

RICE CRUST

3 cups cooked brown rice (cooked without
    salt or fat)
½ cup (2 ounces) shredded reduced-fat
    sharp Cheddar cheese
½ cup fat-free egg substitute
¼ teaspoon salt
Vegetable cooking spray

Combine first 4 ingredients. Press mixture
into bottom and 1 inch up sides of a 13- x 9- x
2-inch baking dish coated with cooking spray.
Yield: 1 crust.

Per serving: Calories 246 (20% from fat)
Fat 5g (Sat 3g   Mono 1g   Poly 1g)
Protein 20g   Carbohydrate 30g   Fiber 3g
Cholesterol 29mg   Sodium 365mg

TURKEY CUTLETS ITALIANO

Count 1 serving as:
½ Starch
1 Meat/Dairy
½ Fat

♥ Good source of
　Potassium

1 pound cubed turkey cutlets, cut into 6
　portions
⅓ cup Italian-seasoned breadcrumbs
Butter-flavored vegetable cooking spray
½ cup canned Italian-seasoned tomato sauce
3 ounces sliced part-skim mozzarella cheese

Dredge cutlets in breadcrumbs, shaking
slightly to remove excess. Place cutlets in a
large nonstick skillet coated with cooking
spray; cook over medium heat until lightly
browned, turning once.

Place cutlets in an 11- x 7- x 1½-inch
baking dish coated with cooking spray. Pour
tomato sauce over cutlets. Bake, uncovered,
at 350° for 15 minutes. Top with mozzarella
cheese, and bake 5 additional minutes or until
cheese melts.
Yield: 6 servings.

Per serving: Calories 173 (30% from fat)
Fat 6g (Sat 2g   Mono 2g   Poly 1g)
Protein 23g   Carbohydrate 7g   Fiber tr
Cholesterol 52mg   Sodium 303mg

TURKEY STROGANOFF

Count 1 serving as:
1 Vegetable
2 Starch
1 Meat/Dairy

♥ Good source of
　Potassium

Vegetable cooking spray
8 ounces sliced fresh mushrooms
½ cup sliced onion
¼ cup chopped celery
1 clove garlic, minced
1 pound turkey cutlets, cut into strips
1 (14½-ounce) can ready-to-serve chicken
　broth
3 tablespoons all-purpose flour
½ teaspoon paprika
¼ teaspoon salt
Dash of ground red pepper
1 (8-ounce) carton low-fat sour cream
3 cups cooked yolk-free egg noodles (cooked
　without salt or fat)

Coat a nonstick skillet with cooking spray;
place over medium heat until hot. Add mushrooms and next 3 ingredients; sauté 5 minutes. Remove from skillet; set aside.

Add turkey to skillet; cook over medium-
high heat until lightly browned, stirring often.
Stir in vegetable mixture; remove from heat.

Combine broth and flour, stirring well. Add
paprika, salt, and pepper, stirring well. Add
broth mixture to turkey mixture in skillet.
Cook over low heat, stirring constantly, until
thickened. Remove from heat. Stir in sour
cream. Serve over noodles.
Yield: 6 servings.

Per serving: Calories 298 (20% from fat)
Fat 7g (Sat 3g   Mono 2g   Poly 1g)
Protein 27g   Carbohydrate 32g   Fiber 2g
Cholesterol 58mg   Sodium 407mg

SALADS

BLUEBERRY-MELON SALAD

Count 1 serving as: 1½ Fruit ½ Fat	♥ Good source of Vitamin C and Potassium

1 medium cantaloupe, peeled and
    cut into 8 rings
8 lettuce leaves
2 cups fresh blueberries
1 cup low-fat sour cream
2 tablespoons brown sugar
¼ teaspoon vanilla extract

Place 1 cantaloupe ring on each of 8 lettuce-lined salad plates. Spoon ¼ cup blueberries into center of each cantaloupe ring.

   Combine sour cream, brown sugar, and vanilla in a small bowl, stirring well with a wire whisk. Top each salad with 2 tablespoons sour cream mixture.
Yield: 8 servings.

Per serving: Calories 115 (19% from fat)
Fat 2g (Sat 1g Mono 1g Poly tr)
Protein 3g Carbohydrate 22g Fiber 2g
Cholesterol 10mg Sodium 45mg

SPICY MELON SALAD

Count 1 serving as: 1 Fruit	♥ Good source of Vitamin C and Potassium

1 cup cubed cantaloupe
1 cup cubed honeydew melon
2 tablespoons fresh lime juice
2 tablespoons honey
¼ teaspoon sweet red pepper flakes
¼ teaspoon ground cardamom
4 red-leaf lettuce leaves

Combine cantaloupe and honeydew in a medium bowl. Combine lime juice and next 3 ingredients, stirring well. Add lime juice mixture to fruit mixture, and toss lightly to coat. Cover and chill at least 1 hour. Serve on lettuce-lined salad plates.
Yield: 4 (½-cup) servings.

Per serving: Calories 64 (3% from fat)
Fat tr (Sat tr Mono 0g Poly tr)
Protein 1g Carbohydrate 17g Fiber 1g
Cholesterol 0mg Sodium 11mg

FRESH FRUIT WITH GINGER-YOGURT DRESSING

Count 1 serving as:	♥ Good source of
2 Fruit	Vitamin C and Potassium

2 cups cubed cantaloupe
2 cups cubed honeydew melon
2 cups sliced fresh strawberries
1 medium Red Delicious apple, chopped
½ cup vanilla nonfat yogurt
2 tablespoons no-sugar-added apricot spread
2 tablespoons orange marmalade
¼ teaspoon ground ginger

Combine first 4 ingredients in a medium bowl. Combine yogurt and remaining 3 ingredients, stirring well. To serve, spoon yogurt mixture over fruit mixture.
Yield: 6 (1-cup) servings.

Per serving: Calories 112 (5% from fat)
Fat 1g (Sat tr Mono tr Poly tr)
Protein 2g Carbohydrate 27g Fiber 3g
Cholesterol tr Sodium 23mg

FRUIT SALAD WITH ORANGE-YOGURT DRESSING

Count 1 serving as:	♥ Good source of
1 Fruit	Vitamin C

2 cups sliced fresh strawberries
1 cup fresh orange sections
½ cup seedless red grapes, halved
1 (8-ounce) can pineapple chunks in juice, drained
¼ cup vanilla low-fat yogurt
¼ cup frozen reduced-calorie whipped topping, thawed
1 teaspoon grated orange rind

Combine first 4 ingredients in a medium bowl. Combine yogurt, whipped topping, and orange rind, stirring well. Add yogurt mixture to fruit mixture, and stir lightly to coat.
Yield: 8 (½-cup) servings.

Per serving: Calories 60 (9% from fat)
Fat 1g (Sat tr Mono tr Poly tr)
Protein 1g Carbohydrate 14g Fiber 2g
Cholesterol tr Sodium 7mg

Marinated Green Bean Salad

Count 1 serving as:
2 Vegetable

1 pound fresh green beans, trimmed and
    broken into 2-inch pieces (3 cups)
1 cup sliced celery
¾ cup chopped sweet red pepper
¼ cup chopped green onions
1 (8¾-ounce) can no-salt-added
    whole-kernel corn, drained
⅓ cup red wine vinegar
2 teaspoons olive oil
½ teaspoon salt
½ teaspoon freshly ground pepper
¼ teaspoon dried oregano
Green leaf lettuce leaves (optional)

Arrange beans in a steamer basket over boiling water; cover and steam 10 minutes or until crisp-tender. Drain and place in ice water until cool; drain.

Combine beans, celery, and next 3 ingredients. Combine vinegar and remaining 4 ingredients in a small bowl, stirring well with a wire whisk. Add vinegar mixture to vegetable mixture, and toss lightly to coat. Cover and chill at least 1 hour. Serve on lettuce leaves, if desired.
Yield: 8 (¾-cup) servings.

Per serving: Calories 55 (23% from fat)
Fat 1g (Sat tr   Mono 1g   Poly tr)
Protein 2g   Carbohydrate 11g   Fiber 3g
Cholesterol 0mg   Sodium 166mg

Recipe pictured on page 109.

Creamy Broccoli Salad

Count 1 serving as: ♥ Good source of
1 Vegetable   Vitamin C
½ Fruit

2 cups bite-size broccoli flowerets
2 cups bite-size cauliflower flowerets
¼ cup chopped purple onion
¼ cup raisins
1 tablespoon chopped pecans
½ cup low-fat mayonnaise
1 tablespoon sugar
1 tablespoon cider vinegar

Combine first 5 ingredients in a large bowl. Combine mayonnaise, sugar, and vinegar, stirring well. Add mayonnaise mixture to broccoli mixture, and toss lightly to coat. Cover and chill at least 1 hour.
Yield: 8 (½-cup) servings.

Per serving: Calories 65 (25% from fat)
Fat 2g (Sat tr   Mono 1g   Poly 1g)
Protein 1g   Carbohydrate 13g   Fiber 2g
Cholesterol 0mg   Sodium 152mg

Italian Broccoli-Cauliflower Salad

Count 1 serving as:
1 Vegetable

♥ Good source of
Vitamin C

2 cups bite-size broccoli flowerets
2 cups bite-size cauliflower flowerets
½ cup chopped purple onion
¼ cup chopped sweet yellow pepper
¼ cup fat-free Italian dressing

Combine first 4 ingredients in a large bowl.
Add dressing to vegetable mixture, and toss
lightly to coat. Cover and chill at least 1 hour.
Yield: 8 (½-cup) servings.

Per serving: Calories 25 (32% from fat)
Fat 1g (Sat tr Mono tr Poly 1g)
Protein 1g Carbohydrate 4g Fiber 2g
Cholesterol tr Sodium 73mg

Cauliflower and Green Pea Salad

Count 1 serving as:
1 Vegetable
½ Starch

1 cup chopped cauliflower
1 cup sliced celery
½ cup chopped green onions
1 (10-ounce) package frozen English peas,
    thawed
¼ cup low-fat sour cream
1 tablespoon chopped fresh parsley
1 tablespoon white vinegar
1 teaspoon Dijon mustard
¼ teaspoon garlic salt
¼ teaspoon cracked black pepper

Combine first 4 ingredients in a large bowl.
Combine sour cream and remaining 5 ingredients in a small bowl, stirring well. Add sour
cream mixture to vegetable mixture, and toss
lightly to coat. Cover and chill.
Yield: 6 (¾-cup) servings.

Per serving: Calories 57 (14% from fat)
Fat 1g (Sat tr Mono tr Poly tr)
Protein 4g Carbohydrate 10g Fiber 3g
Cholesterol 3mg Sodium 122mg

ZESTY CAULIFLOWER SALAD

Count 1 serving as:
2 Vegetable
½ Fat

♥ Good source of
  Vitamin C and
  Potassium

1 medium head cauliflower, chopped
¼ cup chopped green pepper
¼ cup chopped sweet red pepper
½ cup water
¼ cup ketchup
1 tablespoon grated onion
3 tablespoons cider vinegar
1 tablespoon vegetable oil
2 teaspoons sugar

Combine first 3 ingredients in a medium bowl. Combine water and remaining 5 ingredients, stirring well. Add ketchup mixture to vegetable mixture, and toss lightly to coat. Cover and chill at least 2 hours.
Yield: 6 (1-cup) servings.

Per serving: Calories 64 (36% from fat)
Fat 3g (Sat tr Mono 1g Poly 1g)
Protein 2g Carbohydrate 10g Fiber 3g
Cholesterol 0mg Sodium 148mg

TANGY ZUCCHINI SALAD

Count 1 serving as:
2 Vegetable

♥ Good source of
  Vitamin C and
  Potassium

2 cups thinly sliced zucchini
1 cup thinly sliced carrot
1 cup thinly sliced sweet yellow pepper
⅓ cup fat-free Italian dressing
2 tablespoons chopped fresh parsley
¼ teaspoon pepper
3 cups torn romaine lettuce

Combine first 6 ingredients in a large bowl. Cover and chill at least 2 hours. To serve, place ½ cup lettuce on each of 6 salad plates; top each with ⅔ cup vegetable mixture.
Yield: 6 servings.

Per serving: Calories 59 (30% from fat)
Fat 2g (Sat tr Mono 1g Poly 1g)
Protein 1g Carbohydrate 10g Fiber 2g
Cholesterol tr Sodium 130mg

GREEK POTATO SALAD

Count 1 serving as:
1 Starch

1 pound small round red potatoes
2 tablespoons sliced ripe olives
2 tablespoons red wine vinegar
1 teaspoon olive oil
½ teaspoon dried oregano
½ teaspoon pepper
¼ teaspoon salt
3 green onions, chopped
1 (4-ounce) jar diced pimiento, drained
¼ cup crumbled feta cheese

Cut potatoes into bite-size pieces, and place in a medium saucepan with water to cover. Bring to a boil; cover, reduce heat, and simmer 20 minutes or until tender. Drain and place in a medium bowl.

Combine olives and next 7 ingredients in a small bowl. Add olive mixture to potato, and toss lightly to coat. Cover and chill at least 1 hour. To serve, add cheese, and toss lightly.
Yield: 8 (½-cup) servings.

Per serving: Calories 73 (23% from fat)
Fat 2g (Sat 1g Mono 1g Poly tr)
Protein 2g Carbohydrate 13g Fiber 1g
Cholesterol 4mg Sodium 149mg

DILLED POTATO AND PEA SALAD

Count 1 serving as:
1½ Starch

♥ Good source of Vitamin C and Potassium

2 pounds small round red potatoes
1 cup frozen English peas, thawed
½ cup chopped sweet red pepper
½ cup chopped green onions
½ cup plain low-fat yogurt
¼ cup low-fat mayonnaise
1 teaspoon dried dillweed
½ teaspoon salt

Cut potatoes into ¼-inch-thick slices, and place in a large saucepan with water to cover. Bring to a boil; cover, reduce heat, and simmer 20 minutes or until tender. Drain and let cool.

Combine potato, peas, red pepper, and onions in a large bowl. Combine yogurt and remaining 3 ingredients, stirring well. Add yogurt mixture to potato mixture; toss lightly to coat. Cover and chill at least 2 hours.
Yield: 8 (¾-cup) servings.

Per serving: Calories 136 (6% from fat)
Fat 1g (Sat tr Mono tr Poly tr)
Protein 4g Carbohydrate 29g Fiber 3g
Cholesterol 1mg Sodium 248mg

Cucumber Salad Dressing

Count 1 serving as:
Free

1 cup low-fat sour cream
2 tablespoons chopped fresh parsley
1 teaspoon Worcestershire sauce
½ teaspoon lemon juice
½ teaspoon prepared horseradish
¼ teaspoon garlic powder
¼ teaspoon salt
2 small cucumbers, peeled and chopped
1 small onion, chopped

Combine all ingredients in container of an electric blender. Cover and process until smooth, stopping once to scrape down sides. Cover and chill at least 2 hours.
Yield: 2½ cups (serving size: 1 tablespoon).

Per serving: Calories 10 (37% from fat)
Fat tr (Sat tr Mono tr Poly tr)
Protein tr Carbohydrate 1g Fiber tr
Cholesterol 2mg Sodium 22mg

Pineapple-Honey Mustard Dressing

Count 1 serving as:
Free

⅓ cup unsweetened pineapple juice
¼ cup lime juice
¼ cup honey
2 tablespoons Dijon mustard
1½ tablespoons soy sauce
¼ teaspoon garlic powder
⅛ teaspoon dried crushed red pepper

Combine all ingredients in a small bowl, stirring well with a wire whisk.
Yield: 1 cup (serving size: 1 tablespoon).

Note: If you use 2 tablespoons dressing, count as ½ Starch.

Per serving: Calories 22 (4% from fat)
Fat tr (Sat tr Mono tr Poly tr)
Protein tr Carbohydrate 6g Fiber tr
Cholesterol 0mg Sodium 122mg

SOUPS

CHEESY POTATO-BROCCOLI SOUP

Count 1 serving as:
1 Vegetable
1 Starch
½ Meat/Dairy

♥ Good source of Vitamin C and Potassium

4 cups cubed round red potato (about 2 pounds)
1 cup thinly sliced carrot
1 cup chopped onion
2 tablespoons chopped fresh parsley
½ teaspoon salt
⅛ teaspoon ground red pepper
2 (13¾-ounce) cans reduced-sodium chicken broth
1 cup (4 ounces) shredded reduced-fat sharp Cheddar cheese
2 (10-ounce) packages frozen chopped broccoli, thawed

Combine first 7 ingredients in a large Dutch oven. Bring to a boil; cover, reduce heat, and simmer 25 to 30 minutes or until vegetables are tender. Remove from heat, and let cool slightly.

Transfer 2 cups vegetable mixture to container of an electric blender. Cover and process until smooth, stopping once to scrape down sides. Add pureed vegetable mixture, cheese, and broccoli to vegetable mixture in Dutch oven, stirring well. Cook over low heat until cheese melts and soup is thoroughly heated. Serve immediately.
Yield: 8 (1¼-cup) servings.

Per serving: Calories 151 (18% from fat)
Fat 3g (Sat 2g   Mono 1g   Poly tr)
Protein 9g   Carbohydrate 24g   Fiber 4g
Cholesterol 8mg   Sodium 271mg

LENTIL SOUP

Count 1 serving as:
1 Vegetable
2 Starch
½ Meat/Dairy
½ Fat

♥ Good source of Vitamin C, Folate, and Potassium

1 tablespoon olive oil
2 cups chopped onion
½ cup chopped carrot
½ cup chopped celery
1 cup dried lentils
1 cup water
¼ cup chopped fresh parsley
½ teaspoon dried thyme
½ teaspoon dried marjoram
1 (14½-ounce) can diced tomatoes, drained
1 (14½-ounce) can ready-to-serve vegetable broth
1 bay leaf
¼ cup sherry
¼ cup plus 1 tablespoon (1¼ ounces) shredded Swiss cheese

Heat oil in a large saucepan over medium heat. Add onion, carrot, and celery, and sauté 2 minutes. Add lentils and next 7 ingredients; cover and cook 45 minutes or until lentils are tender. Add sherry. Remove and discard bay leaf. To serve, ladle soup into individual bowls, and top each serving with 1 tablespoon cheese.
Yield: 5 (1⅓-cup) servings.

Per serving: Calories 260 (20% from fat)
Fat 6g (Sat 2g   Mono 3g   Poly 1g)
Protein 15g   Carbohydrate 35g   Fiber 11g
Cholesterol 6mg   Sodium 440mg

Marinated Green Bean Salad (page 102)

WILD RICE SOUP

Count 1 serving as:
½ Vegetable
1 Starch

♥ Good source of
Potassium

Butter-flavored vegetable cooking spray
1 cup chopped onion
1 cup sliced celery
1 cup sliced fresh mushrooms
1 (14½-ounce) can ready-to-serve chicken
    broth, divided
3 cups skim milk
½ teaspoon pepper
¼ teaspoon salt
¼ cup all-purpose flour
2 cups cooked wild rice (cooked without salt
    or fat)

Coat a large Dutch oven with cooking spray;
place over medium heat until hot. Add onion
and celery, and sauté 3 minutes. Add mushrooms and 2 tablespoons chicken broth; sauté
7 minutes or until tender. Set aside.
    Combine milk, pepper, and salt in a small
bowl. Add flour, stirring with a wire whisk
until blended. Gradually add milk mixture
and remaining chicken broth to vegetable
mixture; cook over medium heat, stirring constantly, until thoroughly heated. Stir in rice;
reduce heat, and simmer, uncovered, 15 minutes, stirring occasionally.
Yield: 9 (¾-cup) servings.

Per serving: Calories 97 (6% from fat)
Fat 1g (Sat tr   Mono tr   Poly tr)
Protein 6g   Carbohydrate 17g   Fiber 1g
Cholesterol 1mg   Sodium 277mg

VEGETARIAN VEGETABLE SOUP

Count 1 serving as:
2 Vegetable
1 Starch

♥ Good source of
Folate and Potassium

---

1 cup sliced celery
1 cup chopped onion
1 cup sliced carrot
3 cups water
½ teaspoon dried basil
¼ teaspoon dried oregano
¼ teaspoon pepper
1 (14½-ounce) can diced tomatoes with
    garlic and onion, drained
1 (14½-ounce) can ready-to-serve
    vegetable broth
1 (9-ounce) package frozen green beans
½ cup elbow macaroni, uncooked
1 (16-ounce) can red kidney beans, rinsed
    and drained

Combine first 10 ingredients in a large Dutch
oven. Bring to a boil; cover, reduce heat, and
simmer 20 minutes or until carrot is crisp-
tender. Add macaroni and red beans; bring to
a boil. Reduce heat to medium, and cook, uncovered, 15 minutes or until macaroni is done.
Yield: 8 (1¼-cup) servings.

Per serving: Calories 123 (4% from fat)
Fat 1g (Sat tr   Mono tr   Poly tr)
Protein 7g   Carbohydrate 24g   Fiber 5g
Cholesterol 0mg   Sodium 436mg

Curried Corn
(page 117)

ZUCCHINI SOUP

Count 1 serving as:
1 Vegetable
½ Fat

♥ Good source of
Potassium

3 cups shredded zucchini
¼ cup chopped onion
¼ teaspoon dry mustard
¼ teaspoon pepper
⅛ teaspoon dried oregano
⅛ teaspoon dried basil
1 (14½-ounce) can ready-to-serve chicken
 broth
¼ cup low-fat sour cream

Combine first 7 ingredients in a medium saucepan. Bring to a boil; cover, reduce heat, and simmer 10 minutes. Let cool slightly.

Transfer mixture to container of an electric blender; cover and process until smooth, stopping once to scrape down sides.

To serve, ladle mixture into 4 individual soup bowls; stir 1 tablespoon sour cream into each serving. Serve immediately.
Yield: 4 (1-cup) servings.

Per serving: Calories 55 (29% from fat)
Fat 2g (Sat 1g   Mono 1g   Poly tr)
Protein 4g   Carbohydrate 6g   Fiber 1g
Cholesterol 5mg   Sodium 345mg

BLACK BEAN-BUTTERNUT SQUASH SOUP

Count 1 serving as:
2 Starch

♥ Good source of
Folate and Potassium

1 cup dried black beans
10 cups water
1 cup chopped onion
1 cup chopped celery
¼ teaspoon pepper
1 clove garlic, minced
1 bay leaf
1 (1-pound) butternut squash, peeled,
 seeded, and cubed
½ teaspoon salt
2 tablespoons low-fat sour cream

Sort and rinse beans; place in a large Dutch oven. Cover with water to depth of 2 inches above beans; let beans soak overnight. (Or bring to a boil, and boil 2 minutes; remove from heat, cover, and let stand 1 hour.)

Drain beans. Add 10 cups water and next 5 ingredients. Bring to a boil; cover, reduce heat, and simmer 2 hours. Remove and discard bay leaf. Add squash and salt. Cover and cook 30 minutes or until squash is tender.

To serve, ladle soup into individual bowls, and top each serving with 1 teaspoon sour cream.
Yield: 6 (1¼-cup) servings.

Per serving: Calories 157 (5% from fat)
Fat 1g (Sat tr   Mono tr   Poly tr)
Protein 8g   Carbohydrate 31g   Fiber 7g
Cholesterol 2mg   Sodium 219mg

NAVY BEAN SOUP

Count 1 serving as:
2 Starch
½ Meat/Dairy

♥ Good source of
Folate and Potassium

1 cup dried navy beans
¼ cup chopped onion
¼ cup chopped lean ham
1 teaspoon dry mustard
1 teaspoon dried dillweed
¼ teaspoon salt

Sort and rinse beans; place in a large Dutch oven. Cover with water to depth of 2 inches above beans; let soak overnight. (Or bring to a boil, and boil 2 minutes; remove from heat, cover, and let stand 1 hour.)
Drain beans. Add water to cover. Bring to a boil; cover, reduce heat, and simmer 1 hour. Add onion and remaining ingredients; cover and cook 1 hour or until beans are tender.
Yield: 4 (1-cup) servings.

Per serving: Calories 190 (6% from fat)
Fat 1g (Sat tr   Mono tr   Poly tr)
Protein 12g   Carbohydrate 33g   Fiber 9g
Cholesterol 4mg   Sodium 248mg

VEGETARIAN CHILI

Count 1 serving as:
2 Vegetable
1½ Starch
½ Fat

♥ Good source of
Vitamin C, Folate,
and Potassium

1½ tablespoons olive oil
1 large onion, chopped
2 cloves garlic, minced
2 (14½-ounce) cans no-salt-added tomatoes, undrained and chopped
1 (8-ounce) can tomato sauce
1 tablespoon ground cumin
2 teaspoons chili powder
1 teaspoon black pepper
½ teaspoon paprika
½ teaspoon hot sauce
⅛ teaspoon ground red pepper
2 medium zucchini, chopped
1 (15-ounce) can black beans, rinsed and drained
1 (15-ounce) can red kidney beans, rinsed and drained
2 cups water

Heat oil in a large Dutch oven over medium heat. Add onion and garlic, and sauté until tender. Add tomatoes and next 8 ingredients; bring to a boil. Cover, reduce heat, and simmer 10 minutes. Add beans and water; bring to a boil. Cover, reduce heat, and simmer 30 minutes. Remove from heat, and let stand 15 minutes.
Yield: 8 (1½-cup) servings.

Per serving: Calories 193 (17% from fat)
Fat 4g (Sat 1g   Mono 2g   Poly 1g)
Protein 10g   Carbohydrate 33g   Fiber 10g
Cholesterol 0mg   Sodium 532mg

CHICKEN-NOODLE SOUP

Count 1 serving as:
1 Vegetable
½ Starch
½ Meat/Dairy

♥ Good source of
Potassium

½ pound skinned, boned chicken breasts,
    cut into bite-size pieces
2 (13¾-ounce) cans reduced-sodium
    chicken broth
2 cups water
1 cup sliced celery
1 cup sliced carrot
1 cup chopped onion
1 teaspoon dried dillweed
½ teaspoon lemon-pepper seasoning
¼ teaspoon dry mustard
3 ounces linguine, uncooked and broken
    in half

Combine first 9 ingredients in a large Dutch
oven. Bring to a boil; cover, reduce heat, and
simmer 45 minutes. Add pasta; cover and
cook 12 minutes or until pasta is tender.
Yield: 6 (1⅓-cup) servings.

Per serving: Calories 123 (14% from fat)
Fat 2g (Sat 1g   Mono 1g   Poly tr)
Protein 11g   Carbohydrate 15g   Fiber 2g
Cholesterol 21mg   Sodium 376mg

VEGETABLE BEEF SOUP

Count 1 serving as:
1 Vegetable
1 Starch
½ Meat/Dairy

♥ Good source of
Vitamin C and
Potassium

Olive oil-flavored vegetable cooking spray
1 pound lean beef tips
2 cups cubed red potato
1 cup sliced celery
1 cup chopped onion
1 cup sliced carrot
¼ teaspoon pepper
2 (14½-ounce) cans ready-to-serve beef
    broth
2 (14½-ounce) cans stewed tomatoes,
    undrained
1 (10-ounce) package frozen whole-kernel
    corn
1 (10-ounce) package frozen green beans

Coat a large Dutch oven with cooking spray;
place over medium heat until hot. Add beef,
and cook until browned on all sides. Drain
beef, and pat dry with paper towels. Wipe
drippings from Dutch oven with a paper towel.
    Return beef to Dutch oven. Add potato and
remaining ingredients; bring to a boil. Cover,
reduce heat, and simmer 45 minutes or until
beef is tender.
Yield: 9 (1½-cup) servings.

Per serving: Calories 158 (11% from fat)
Fat 2g (Sat 1g   Mono 1g   Poly tr)
Protein 14g   Carbohydrate 23g   Fiber 4g
Cholesterol 24mg   Sodium 431mg

VEGETABLES

ITALIAN-STYLE GREEN BEANS

Count 1 serving as:
1½ Vegetable

1 pound fresh green beans, trimmed and cut
  into 2-inch pieces
1 (14½-ounce) can Italian-style diced
  tomatoes, undrained
1 large sweet onion, sliced
¼ teaspoon salt

Combine all ingredients in a Dutch oven. Bring
to a boil; cover, reduce heat, and simmer 20 to
25 minutes or until beans are tender.
Yield: 6 (¾-cup) servings.

Per serving: Calories 38 (7% from fat)
Fat tr (Sat tr   Mono tr   Poly tr)
Protein 2g   Carbohydrate 9g   Fiber 3g
Cholesterol 0mg   Sodium 215mg

MINTED CARROTS

Count 1 serving as:
2 Vegetable

1 (16-ounce) package baby carrots
1 teaspoon cornstarch
⅓ cup water
2 teaspoons honey
½ teaspoon dried mint

Place carrots in a medium saucepan, and add
water to cover. Bring to a boil; cover, reduce
heat, and cook 10 minutes or until tender.
Drain carrots; transfer to a serving bowl, and
keep warm.
  Combine cornstarch and water in a small
saucepan, and cook over medium heat, stirring constantly, until thickened. Stir in honey
and mint. Pour cornstarch mixture over carrots, and stir until coated.
Yield: 4 (¾-cup) servings.

Per serving: Calories 60 (3% from fat)
Fat tr (Sat tr   Mono tr   Poly tr)
Protein 1g   Carbohydrate 14g   Fiber 3g
Cholesterol 0mg   Sodium 69mg

CAJUN CAULIFLOWER MEDLEY

Count 1 serving as:
1 Vegetable

♥ Good source of Vitamin C and Potassium

4 cups cauliflower flowerets
2 cups sliced zucchini
½ cup sliced fresh mushrooms
⅓ cup thinly sliced onion
¼ cup chopped green pepper
2 tablespoons chopped fresh parsley
¼ teaspoon dried rosemary
¼ teaspoon pepper
1 (14½-ounce) can Cajun-style stewed
    tomatoes, undrained
1 clove garlic, crushed

Combine all ingredients in a medium saucepan. Bring to a boil; cover, reduce heat, and simmer 15 minutes or until vegetables are tender.
Yield: 8 (½-cup) servings.

Per serving: Calories 38 (7% from fat)
Fat tr (Sat tr Mono tr Poly tr)
Protein 2g Carbohydrate 8g Fiber 3g
Cholesterol 0mg Sodium 214mg

CURRIED CORN

Count 1 serving as:
1 Starch
½ Fat

4 medium ears fresh corn
1 tablespoon plus 1 teaspoon
    reduced-calorie margarine, melted
½ teaspoon curry powder

Remove husks and silks from corn. Place corn in a large Dutch oven with boiling water to cover. Cover and cook 6 to 7 minutes or until tender. Drain and place corn in a serving dish. Combine margarine and curry powder in a small bowl. Drizzle evenly over corn.
Yield: 4 servings.

Per serving: Calories 101 (26% from fat)
Fat 3g (Sat tr Mono 1g Poly 1g)
Protein 3g Carbohydrate 20g Fiber 2g
Cholesterol 0mg Sodium 60mg

Recipe pictured on page 110.

POTATOES WITH GREEN ONIONS

Count 1 serving as:
1½ Starch

♥ Good source of Potassium

1½ pounds small round red potatoes, cut into quarters
½ cup canned ready-to-serve chicken broth
¼ teaspoon pepper
6 green onions, chopped

Place potato in a single layer in a large non-stick Dutch oven; add broth, and sprinkle with pepper. Bring to a boil; cover, reduce heat, and simmer 20 minutes or until tender. Add green onions, and cook, uncovered, until liquid evaporates, stirring occasionally.
Yield: 6 (¾-cup) servings.

Per serving: Calories 106 (2% from fat)
Fat tr (Sat tr   Mono tr   Poly tr)
Protein 3g   Carbohydrate 24g   Fiber 3g
Cholesterol 0mg   Sodium 74mg

CURRIED POTATOES AND PEPPERS

Count 1 serving as:
1 Vegetable
½ Starch

♥ Good source of Vitamin C

---

8 small round red potatoes, cut into quarters
2 medium onions, each cut into 6 wedges
1 sweet red pepper, seeded and cut into 1-inch pieces
1 green pepper, seeded and cut into 1-inch pieces
Vegetable cooking spray
½ teaspoon garlic powder
½ teaspoon curry powder
¼ teaspoon salt

Place first 4 ingredients on a baking sheet coated with cooking spray. Coat vegetables lightly with cooking spray. Combine garlic powder, curry powder, and salt in a small bowl; sprinkle evenly over vegetables. Bake at 425° for 45 minutes or until tender, stirring occasionally.
Yield: 8 (1-cup) servings.

Per serving: Calories 60 (2% from fat)
Fat tr (Sat tr   Mono tr   Poly tr)
Protein 1g   Carbohydrate 14g   Fiber 2g
Cholesterol 0mg   Sodium 76mg

ROASTED POTATOES AND CARROTS

Count 1 serving as:
½ Vegetable
1 Starch

♥ Good source of Potassium

1¼ pounds small round red potatoes, thinly sliced
1 (16-ounce) package baby carrots
Olive oil-flavored vegetable cooking spray
1 teaspoon dried parsley flakes
½ teaspoon salt
¼ teaspoon garlic powder
¼ teaspoon pepper

Place potato and carrots on a baking sheet coated with cooking spray. Coat vegetables lightly with cooking spray. Combine parsley flakes and remaining 3 ingredients, and sprinkle evenly over vegetables. Bake at 400° for 45 to 50 minutes or until vegetables are tender, stirring occasionally.
Yield: 8 (⅔-cup) servings.

Per serving: Calories 86 (2% from fat)
Fat tr (Sat tr   Mono tr   Poly tr)
Protein 6g   Carbohydrate 17g   Fiber 3g
Cholesterol 2mg   Sodium 185mg

BAKED POTATOES WITH CREAM CHEESE TOPPING

Count 1 serving as:
1 Starch

♥ Good source of Potassium

4 medium baking potatoes (about 1¾ pounds)
4 ounces nonfat cream cheese
½ cup 1% low-fat cottage cheese
2 teaspoons fresh or frozen chives
½ teaspoon dried parsley flakes
¼ teaspoon salt
⅛ teaspoon garlic powder
Dash of ground red pepper

Pierce skin of each potato with a fork 2 times. Place potatoes on oven rack, and bake at 350° for 1 hour or until tender. Cut each potato in half lengthwise, and fluff with a fork. Set aside.
  Position knife blade in food processor bowl; add cream cheese and cottage cheese. Process until smooth. Stir in chives and remaining 4 ingredients. Top potato halves evenly with cream cheese mixture.
Yield: 8 servings.

Per serving: Calories 91 (4% from fat)
Fat tr (Sat tr   Mono tr   Poly tr)
Protein 5g   Carbohydrate 17g   Fiber 1g
Cholesterol 1mg   Sodium 221mg

HORSERADISH MASHED POTATOES

Count 1 serving as:
1 Starch

♥ Good source of
Potassium

1¼ pounds baking potatoes, peeled and
    sliced
⅓ cup skim milk
1 tablespoon prepared horseradish
2 teaspoons dried chives
½ teaspoon salt
⅛ teaspoon pepper

Place potato in a medium saucepan; add
water to cover. Bring to a boil; cover, reduce
heat, and simmer 20 minutes or until potato
is tender. Drain.
   Transfer cooked potato to a large bowl. Beat
at medium speed of an electric mixer until
smooth. Add milk and remaining ingredients,
and beat well.
Yield: 6 (½-cup) servings.

Per serving: Calories 79 (1% from fat)
Fat tr (Sat tr   Mono tr   Poly tr)
Protein 2g   Carbohydrate 18g   Fiber 2g
Cholesterol tr   Sodium 207mg

SWEET POTATO CASSEROLE

Count 1 serving as:
1½ Starch

♥ Good source of
Potassium

1 pound sweet potatoes, peeled and cubed
¼ teaspoon ground cinnamon
2 ounces light process cream cheese,
    softened
¼ cup firmly packed brown sugar
¼ cup canned crushed pineapple in juice,
    drained
½ teaspoon vanilla extract
Butter-flavored vegetable cooking spray
1 tablespoon finely chopped pecans

Place potato in a large saucepan with water to
cover. Bring to a boil; reduce heat to medium,
and cook, uncovered, until tender. Drain and
let cool.
   Place potato in a medium bowl. Add cinnamon, and beat at medium speed of an electric
mixer until smooth. Add cream cheese, brown
sugar, pineapple, and vanilla; beat well.
   Transfer potato mixture to a 1-quart baking
dish coated with cooking spray. Top with
pecans. Bake at 350° for 20 minutes or until
thoroughly heated.
Yield: 6 (½-cup) servings.

Per serving: Calories 129 (19% from fat)
Fat 3g (Sat 1g   Mono 1g   Poly tr)
Protein 2g   Carbohydrate 25g   Fiber 2g
Cholesterol 3mg   Sodium 63mg

LEMON-PEPPER SPINACH

Count 1 serving as:
1 Vegetable

♥ Good source of Vitamin C, Folate, and Potassium

1 (10-ounce) package fresh spinach
⅓ cup water
¾ teaspoon lemon-pepper seasoning
2 lemon wedges

Rinse spinach in cold water, and drain. Place spinach and ⅓ cup water in a large saucepan. Bring to a boil; cover and cook over medium heat 2 to 3 minutes or until spinach is tender. Add lemon-pepper seasoning, and toss well. Top with lemon wedges. Serve immediately.
Yield: 2 (½-cup) servings.

Per serving. Calories 28 (13% from fat)
Fat tr (Sat tr Mono tr Poly tr)
Protein 3g Carbohydrate 5g Fiber 3g
Cholesterol 0mg Sodium 210mg

SPANISH SQUASH

Count 1 serving as:
2 Vegetable

♥ Good source of Vitamin C and Potassium

2 pounds yellow squash, sliced
¼ cup chopped onion
¼ cup water
¼ teaspoon salt
Dash of ground red pepper
2 medium tomatoes, chopped
1 (4½-ounce) can diced green chiles, drained
¼ cup (1 ounce) shredded reduced-fat sharp Cheddar cheese

Combine first 3 ingredients in a medium saucepan. Bring to a boil; cover, reduce heat to medium, and cook 10 minutes or until squash is crisp-tender. Drain; stir in salt and red pepper.

Spoon squash mixture into a 1½-quart baking dish. Top squash mixture with tomato. Sprinkle with green chiles, and top with cheese. Bake at 400° for 5 minutes or until cheese melts.
Yield: 8 (¾-cup) servings.

Per serving: Calories 46 (21% from fat)
Fat 1g (Sat tr Mono tr Poly tr)
Protein 2g Carbohydrate 8g Fiber 2g
Cholesterol 2mg Sodium 262mg

VEGETABLE-STUFFED YELLOW SQUASH

Count 1 serving as:
1 Vegetable
1 Starch

♥ Good source of Vitamin C and Potassium

6 medium-size yellow squash
Vegetable cooking spray
1 cup chopped fresh mushrooms
½ cup chopped onion
½ cup chopped green pepper
½ cup chopped celery
2 cups chopped tomato
1 cup cooked barley (cooked without salt or fat)
¼ teaspoon pepper
⅛ teaspoon salt
½ cup (2 ounces) shredded reduced-fat sharp Cheddar cheese
⅛ teaspoon paprika

Place squash in a 13- x 9- x 2-inch baking dish coated with vegetable cooking spray. Bake at 350° for 30 minutes or until squash is tender. Drain squash, if necessary. Let squash cool 10 minutes.

Cut each squash in half lengthwise; scoop out pulp from each squash half, and place pulp in a bowl. Set pulp aside. Return squash shells to baking dish, and set aside.

Coat a large nonstick skillet with vegetable cooking spray. Add chopped mushrooms, chopped onion, chopped green pepper, and chopped celery; sauté 5 to 6 minutes or until vegetables are tender. Add mushroom mixture to squash pulp. Stir in tomato, barley, pepper, and salt.

Spoon vegetable mixture evenly into squash shells. Top shells evenly with shredded Cheddar cheese and paprika. Bake at 350° for 5 minutes or until cheese melts.
Yield: 6 servings (serving size: 2 stuffed squash halves).

Per serving: Calories 109 (18% from fat)
Fat 2g (Sat 1g   Mono tr   Poly tr)
Protein 6g   Carbohydrate 19g   Fiber 25g
Cholesterol 5mg   Sodium 206mg

SUMMER SQUASH CASSEROLE

Count 1 serving as:
1 Vegetable
1 Starch
½ Fat

♥ Good source of Potassium

1½ pounds yellow squash, sliced
1¼ cups chopped onion
1 cup shredded carrot
½ cup diced celery
⅔ cup water
¾ cup fine, dry breadcrumbs
½ teaspoon dried sage
¼ teaspoon dried thyme
¼ teaspoon dried rosemary
Butter-flavored vegetable cooking spray
½ cup (2 ounces) shredded reduced-fat sharp Cheddar cheese
1 teaspoon dried parsley flakes

Combine first 5 ingredients in a large saucepan. Bring to a boil; cover, reduce heat to medium, and cook 10 minutes or until crisp-tender. Remove from heat, and drain. Stir in breadcrumbs and next 3 ingredients.

Spoon squash mixture into a 1-quart baking dish coated with cooking spray. Top with cheese and parsley. Bake at 350° for 20 minutes or until thoroughly heated.
Yield: 6 (½-cup) servings.

Per serving: Calories 116 (19% from fat)
Fat 2g (Sat 1g   Mono 1g   Poly tr)
Protein 6g   Carbohydrate 19g   Fiber 3g
Cholesterol 5mg   Sodium 274mg

BAKED TOMATOES WITH SPINACH

Count 1 serving as:
1 Vegetable

♥ Good source of Potassium

1 (10-ounce) package frozen chopped spinach
Butter-flavored vegetable cooking spray
2 tablespoons chopped onion
1 clove garlic, minced
2 tablespoons crumbled feta cheese
½ teaspoon dried basil
¼ teaspoon salt
3 medium tomatoes

Cook spinach according to package directions, omitting salt and fat. Drain thoroughly, and set aside.

Coat a medium nonstick skillet with cooking spray. Add onion and garlic; sauté until tender. Stir in spinach, cheese, basil, and salt. Remove from heat, and set aside.

Cut each tomato in half crosswise. Top tomato halves evenly with spinach mixture. Place in an 11- x 7- x 1½-inch baking dish. Bake, uncovered, at 350° for 20 minutes.
Yield: 6 servings.

Per serving: Calories 35 (25% from fat)
Fat 1g (Sat 1g   Mono tr   Poly tr)
Protein 2g   Carbohydrate 6g   Fiber 2g
Cholesterol 3mg   Sodium 165mg

BAKED GREEK ZUCCHINI

Count 1 serving as:
1½ Vegetable
½ Fat

♥ Good source of
   Potassium

4 cups shredded zucchini (about 4 medium)
¼ cup crumbled basil- and tomato-flavored
    feta cheese
¼ teaspoon salt
1 egg, lightly beaten
1 egg white, lightly beaten
Vegetable cooking spray
¼ cup grated Romano cheese

Press zucchini between paper towels to remove excess moisture. Combine zucchini, feta cheese, and next 3 ingredients.

  Spoon mixture into a 9-inch pieplate coated with cooking spray. Top with Romano cheese. Cover and bake at 350° for 30 minutes. Uncover and bake 10 minutes or until mixture is set. Let stand 10 minutes before slicing into wedges.
Yield: 6 servings.

Note: You can use ¼ cup crumbled plain feta cheese plus ½ teaspoon dried basil if the basil- and tomato-flavored kind is not available.

Per serving: Calories 69 (44% from fat)
Fat 3g (Sat 2g   Mono 1g   Poly tr)
Protein 4g   Carbohydrate 6g   Fiber 2g
Cholesterol 45mg   Sodium 231mg

SPECIAL
OCCASION

Grasshopper Pie

Count 1 serving as:
1½ Starch
1 Fat

⅓ cup cold water
1 envelope unflavored gelatin
3½ cups miniature marshmallows
⅓ cup skim milk
¼ cup crème de menthe
¼ cup white crème de cacao
1 (12-ounce) container frozen reduced-
   calorie whipped topping, thawed
¾ cup crushed chocolate wafers (about
   12 wafers)

Combine water and gelatin in top of a double boiler, and let stand 1 minute. Add marshmallows and milk to gelatin mixture. Place double boiler over simmering water, and cook until marshmallows melt, stirring occasionally.
   Remove from heat, and stir in liqueurs. Let mixture cool slightly (do not let mixture thicken). Fold in whipped topping.
   Spread wafer crumbs in bottom of an 11- x 7- x 1½-inch baking dish, reserving 1 tablespoon crumbs. Spoon topping mixture evenly over crumbs in dish. Sprinkle remaining 1 tablespoon crumbs over topping mixture. Cover and chill at least 2 hours or until set.
Yield: 12 servings.

Per serving: Calories 172 (27% from fat)
Fat 5g (Sat 4g   Mono 1g   Poly tr)
Protein 2g   Carbohydrate 28g   Fiber tr
Cholesterol 1mg   Sodium 53mg

Banana Ice Cream

Count 1 serving as: ♥ Good source of
1 Fruit   Potassium
½ Starch
½ Meat/Dairy

1 quart 2% low-fat milk
1½ cups fat-free egg substitute
¾ cup sugar
1 (12-ounce) can evaporated skimmed milk
6 large ripe bananas, peeled and mashed
2 tablespoons lemon juice
1 tablespoon vanilla extract

Combine first 4 ingredients in a large bowl. Add mashed banana, lemon juice, and vanilla, stirring well.
   Pour mixture into freezer container of a 6-quart hand-turned or electric freezer. Freeze according to manufacturer's instructions. Pack freezer with additional ice and rock salt, and let stand 1 hour before serving.
Yield: 16 (1-cup) servings.

Per serving: Calories 142 (9% from fat)
Fat 1g (Sat 1g   Mono tr   Poly tr)
Protein 6g   Carbohydrate 27g   Fiber 1g
Cholesterol 5mg   Sodium 90mg

BAKED TROPICAL FRUIT

Count 1 serving as:
1½ Fruit

3 ripe peaches, peeled and sliced
2 large ripe bananas, peeled and sliced
1 ripe mango, peeled and sliced
1 (15½-ounce) can pineapple chunks in juice, drained
Vegetable cooking spray
¼ cup firmly packed brown sugar
½ cup unsweetened applesauce
1 tablespoon butter-flavored granules
1 teaspoon curry powder

Combine first 4 ingredients in an 11- x 7- x 1½-inch baking dish coated with cooking spray. Combine brown sugar, applesauce, butter-flavored granules, and curry powder, and spread over fruit.

Bake, uncovered, at 350° for 30 minutes or until fruit is tender and mixture is hot and bubbly.
Yield: 12 (½-cup) servings.

Per serving: Calories 87 (2% from fat)
Fat tr (Sat tr Mono tr Poly tr)
Protein 1g Carbohydrate 22g Fiber 2g
Cholesterol 0mg Sodium 25mg

POACHED FRUIT MEDLEY

Count 1 serving as:
1½ Fruit

4 ripe peaches
2 cups water
¼ cup sugar
¼ cup fresh lime juice
2 tablespoons sweet white wine (Riesling)
2 cups seedless green grapes
1 cup fresh raspberries

Place peaches in boiling water to cover for about 10 seconds to loosen skins. Immerse peaches in cold water immediately. Remove and discard skins.

Place 2 cups water and sugar in a Dutch oven, and bring to a boil. Add lime juice and wine. Add peaches; reduce heat, and simmer, uncovered, 10 minutes, turning peaches occasionally. Remove peaches from liquid with a slotted spoon, and set aside. Let cool to room temperature.

Cook lime juice mixture in Dutch oven over medium-high heat until reduced to 1 cup. Let cool to room temperature.

Slice peaches. Combine peaches, grapes, and raspberries; add lime juice mixture, and stir lightly. Serve at room temperature or chilled.
Yield: 8 (⅔-cup) servings.

Per serving: Calories 83 (4% from fat)
Fat tr (Sat tr Mono tr Poly tr)
Protein 1g Carbohydrate 21g Fiber 2g
Cholesterol 0mg Sodium 3mg

Whole Wheat Carrot Cake (page 133)

Orange Crêpes

Count 1 serving as:
1 Fruit
1 Starch
½ Meat/Dairy

♥ Good source of Vitamin C and Potassium

1 cup all-purpose flour
1 cup skim milk
½ cup fat-free egg substitute
1 tablespoon vegetable oil
½ teaspoon vanilla extract
8 ounces nonfat cream cheese, softened
¼ cup sugar, divided
½ teaspoon grated orange rind, divided
1 cup plus 2 tablespoons unsweetened
    orange juice, divided
1 tablespoon cornstarch
Vegetable cooking spray
4 oranges, peeled and sectioned

Combine first 5 ingredients in a medium bowl, stirring with a wire whisk until smooth. Set aside.

Combine cream cheese, 2 tablespoons sugar, ¼ teaspoon orange rind, and 2 tablespoons orange juice in a small bowl, and stir until smooth. Set aside.

Combine remaining 2 tablespoons sugar, ¼ teaspoon orange rind, 1 cup orange juice, and cornstarch in a medium saucepan, stirring well. Cook over medium heat, stirring constantly, until mixture is thickened and clear. Remove from heat, and let cool.

Coat bottom of a 6-inch crêpe pan or heavy skillet with vegetable cooking spray; place over medium heat until hot. Pour 3 tablespoons batter into pan, and quickly tilt pan in all directions so batter covers bottom of pan. Cook 1 minute or until crêpe can be shaken loose from pan. Turn crêpe, and cook about 30 seconds. Place crêpe on a towel to cool. Repeat with remaining batter. (Do not stack crêpes.)

Spread about 1 tablespoon cream cheese mixture on each crêpe, and fold into quarters. Place folded crêpes in a 13- x 9- x 2-inch baking dish, overlapping crêpes. Gently stir orange sections into cooled orange syrup mixture. Pour syrup mixture over crêpes, and bake at 350° for 20 minutes or until crêpes are thoroughly heated.

Yield: 8 servings (serving size: 2 crêpes).

Per serving: Calories 188 (10% from fat)
Fat 2g (Sat tr   Mono 1g   Poly 1g)
Protein 9g   Carbohydrate 34g   Fiber 2g
Cholesterol 1mg   Sodium 208mg

Rice Pudding

Count 1 serving as:
1 Fruit
2 Starch

1 cup brown rice, uncooked
2 cups water
1 teaspoon grated orange rind
¼ teaspoon salt
2 cups skim milk
⅓ cup sugar
⅓ cup golden raisins
½ teaspoon ground cinnamon, divided

Combine first 4 ingredients in a 3-quart saucepan. Bring to a boil; cover, reduce heat, and simmer 40 minutes or until rice is tender and liquid is absorbed.

Combine rice mixture, milk, sugar, raisins, and ¼ teaspoon cinnamon. Place in a 1½-quart baking dish. Sprinkle with remaining ¼ teaspoon cinnamon. Cover and bake at 350° for 30 minutes. Serve warm or chilled.
Yield: 6 (⅔-cup) servings.

Per serving: Calories 212 (5% from fat)
Fat 1g (Sat tr Mono tr Poly tr)
Protein 6g Carbohydrate 46g Fiber 2g
Cholesterol 1mg Sodium 146mg

Lemon-Glazed Apple Betty

Count 1 serving as:
½ Fruit
2 Starch
½ Fat

3 large Golden Delicious apples, cored and
    sliced
½ cup water
Vegetable cooking spray
¼ cup all-purpose flour
¼ teaspoon baking powder
½ cup sugar
¼ cup chopped pecans
¼ cup unsweetened applesauce
2 teaspoons vanilla extract
1 egg, lightly beaten
¼ cup sifted powdered sugar
½ teaspoon grated lemon rind
2 teaspoons fresh lemon juice
2⅔ cups vanilla nonfat frozen yogurt
¼ teaspoon ground cinnamon

Place apple and water in an 11- x 7- x 1½-inch baking dish coated with cooking spray. Combine flour and next 6 ingredients, and pour over apples. Bake at 375° for 45 minutes.

Combine powdered sugar, lemon rind, and lemon juice, stirring well. Spread glaze over hot apple mixture. Serve warm. Top each serving with ⅓ cup frozen yogurt, and sprinkle with cinnamon.
Yield: 8 servings.

Per serving: Calories 206 (18% from fat)
Fat 4g (Sat 1g Mono 2g Poly 1g)
Protein 4g Carbohydrate 40g Fiber 2g
Cholesterol 26mg Sodium 56mg

APPLE COBBLER

Count 1 serving as:
1 Fruit
1½ Starch
½ Fat

4 cups chopped apple
2 cups water, divided
¾ cup sugar, divided
1 teaspoon ground cinnamon
2 tablespoons cornstarch
1 cup all-purpose flour
1½ teaspoons baking powder
½ cup skim milk
2 tablespoons vegetable oil
½ teaspoon vanilla extract

Combine apple, 1 cup water, ½ cup sugar, and cinnamon in a large saucepan. Bring to a boil; reduce heat, and simmer, uncovered, 5 minutes. Combine cornstarch and remaining 1 cup water, and stir into apple mixture. Bring to a boil, and cook 1 minute. Spoon apple mixture into a 13- x 9- x 2-inch baking dish. Set aside.

Combine flour, baking powder, and remaining ¼ cup sugar. Combine milk, oil, and vanilla; add to flour mixture, stirring just until dry ingredients are moistened. Pour batter over apple mixture in baking dish. Bake at 350° for 25 to 30 minutes or until lightly browned.
Yield: 8 servings.

Per serving: Calories 206 (16% from fat)
Fat 4g (Sat tr Mono 2g Poly 1g)
Protein 2g Carbohydrate 42g Fiber 2g
Cholesterol tr Sodium 100mg

CHOCOLATE POUND CAKE

Count 1 serving as:
1 Starch
1 Fat

1 cup sugar
½ cup margarine
2½ cups all-purpose flour
1 teaspoon baking powder
¾ teaspoon baking soda
¼ teaspoon salt
¼ cup unsweetened cocoa
1⅓ cups nonfat buttermilk
1 teaspoon vanilla extract
Vegetable cooking spray

Combine sugar and margarine in a large bowl; beat at medium speed of an electric mixer until fluffy.

Combine flour and next 4 ingredients; add to creamed mixture alternately with buttermilk, beginning and ending with flour mixture. Stir in vanilla.

Spoon batter into a 10-inch Bundt pan coated with cooking spray. Bake at 350° for 40 minutes or until a wooden pick inserted in center comes out clean. Let cake cool in pan 5 minutes. Remove from pan, and let cool completely on a wire rack.
Yield: 24 servings.

Per serving: Calories 122 (31% from fat)
Fat 4g (Sat 1g Mono 2g Poly 1g)
Protein 2g Carbohydrate 20g Fiber 1g
Cholesterol tr Sodium 143mg

WHOLE WHEAT CARROT CAKE

Count 1 serving as:
½ Vegetable
2 Starch

1 teaspoon margarine
2 tablespoons finely chopped pecans
2 tablespoons nutlike cereal nuggets (such as Grape-Nuts)
2 cups whole wheat flour
1½ teaspoons baking powder
1 teaspoon baking soda
¼ teaspoon salt
1 teaspoon ground cinnamon
1 cup fat-free egg substitute
1 cup honey
½ cup unsweetened applesauce
1 teaspoon vanilla extract
4 cups shredded carrot
Vegetable cooking spray
Cream Cheese Frosting

Melt margarine in a small nonstick skillet over medium-high heat. Add pecans and cereal, and sauté 3 minutes. Set aside. Combine flour and next 4 ingredients in a large bowl. Add egg substitute and next 3 ingredients to dry mixture; stir well. Stir in pecan mixture and carrot.

Pour batter into a 13- x 9- x 2-inch pan coated with cooking spray. Bake at 350° for 25 to 30 minutes or until a wooden pick inserted in center comes out clean. Let cool in pan on a wire rack. Spread Cream Cheese Frosting evenly over top of cake.
Yield: 18 servings.

CREAM CHEESE FROSTING

4 ounces light process cream cheese, chilled
1 cup sifted powdered sugar
½ teaspoon vanilla extract

Combine all ingredients in a medium bowl. Beat at high speed of an electric mixer until smooth.
Yield: ¾ cup.

Per serving: Calories 172 (12% from fat)
Fat 2g (Sat 1g Mono 1g Poly tr)
Protein 4g Carbohydrate 37g Fiber 3g
Cholesterol 2mg Sodium 210mg

Recipe pictured on page 128.

LEMON CAKE

½ cup sugar
¼ cup unsweetened applesauce
2 tablespoons vegetable oil
1 teaspoon grated lemon rind
2 teaspoons fresh lemon juice
1 egg yolk, lightly beaten
⅔ cup all-purpose flour
½ teaspoon baking powder
¼ teaspoon baking soda
⅛ teaspoon salt
2 egg whites
Vegetable cooking spray
½ cup sifted powdered sugar
1 teaspoon fresh lemon juice
1 teaspoon water

Combine first 6 ingredients in a large bowl. Combine flour and next 3 ingredients. Add flour mixture to applesauce mixture; stir well. Beat egg whites at high speed of an electric mixer until stiff peaks form. Fold into batter.

Spoon batter into an 8-inch square pan coated with cooking spray. Bake at 350° for 20 to 22 minutes or until cake is lightly browned and a wooden pick inserted in center comes out clean. Remove from pan, and let cool on a wire rack.

Combine powdered sugar, 1 teaspoon lemon juice, and water in a small bowl. Drizzle over cooled cake, and cut cake into squares.
Yield: 9 servings.

Per serving: Calories 143 (23% from fat)
Fat 4g (Sat tr Mono 2g Poly 1g)
Protein 2g Carbohydrate 26g Fiber tr
Cholesterol 24mg Sodium 107mg

CITRUS LOAF

1 cup sugar
1 cup plain nonfat yogurt
½ cup unsweetened applesauce
1 teaspoon vanilla extract
2 eggs, lightly beaten
1 cup all-purpose flour
1 cup whole wheat flour
1 teaspoon baking powder
¼ teaspoon baking soda
¼ teaspoon salt
1 tablespoon grated lime rind
1 tablespoon plus 2 teaspoons grated orange rind, divided
Butter-flavored vegetable cooking spray
¼ cup sifted powdered sugar
2 teaspoons fresh lime juice
¼ teaspoon vanilla extract
¼ teaspoon butter flavoring

Combine first 5 ingredients in a bowl. Combine all-purpose flour and next 4 ingredients; add to applesauce mixture, stirring just until dry ingredients are moistened. Fold in lime rind and 1 tablespoon orange rind. Pour into a 9- x 5- x 3-inch loafpan coated with cooking spray. Bake at 350° for 45 minutes.

Combine remaining 2 teaspoons orange rind, powdered sugar, and remaining 3 ingredients; stirring until smooth. Drizzle over loaf. Let cool in pan 15 minutes; remove from pan. Let cool completely on a wire rack.
Yield: 16 servings.

Per serving: Calories 132 (6% from fat)
Fat 1g (Sat tr Mono tr Poly tr)
Protein 3g Carbohydrate 28g Fiber 1g
Cholesterol 24mg Sodium 106mg

CARROT COOKIES

Count 1 serving as:
1 Starch

1 (14-ounce) can sliced carrots, drained
½ cup sugar
½ cup unsweetened applesauce
½ cup dark corn syrup
¼ cup fat-free egg substitute
2 tablespoons vegetable oil
1 teaspoon vanilla extract
1¼ cups all-purpose flour
¾ cup whole wheat flour
2 teaspoons baking powder
¼ teaspoon salt
1 teaspoon ground cinnamon
Vegetable cooking spray
¾ cup sifted powdered sugar
1 tablespoon unsweetened orange juice
¼ teaspoon ground cinnamon

Combine first 7 ingredients in a medium bowl; beat at medium speed of an electric mixer until blended. Combine all-purpose flour and next 4 ingredients; add to carrot mixture, stirring just until dry ingredients are moistened. Drop by teaspoonfuls 1 inch apart onto baking sheets coated with cooking spray. Bake at 375° for 12 minutes.

Transfer cookies to wire racks. Combine powdered sugar, orange juice, and ¼ teaspoon cinnamon in a shallow bowl. Dip tops of warm cookies in glaze mixture; return cookies to racks to cool completely.
Yield: 5 dozen (serving size: 2 cookies).

Per serving: Calories 83 (11% from fat)
Fat 1g (Sat tr   Mono 1g   Poly tr)
Protein 1g   Carbohydrate 18g   Fiber 1g
Cholesterol 0mg   Sodium 78mg

OATMEAL RAISIN COOKIES

Count 1 serving as:
1 Starch
½ Fat

⅓ cup firmly packed brown sugar
¼ cup unsweetened applesauce
¼ cup margarine
¼ cup fat-free egg substitute
1 teaspoon vanilla extract
⅔ cup all-purpose flour
⅓ cup whole wheat flour
½ teaspoon baking soda
¼ teaspoon salt
¾ cup regular oats, uncooked
½ cup raisins
Vegetable cooking spray
1 tablespoon sugar
1 teaspoon ground cinnamon

Combine first 3 ingredients in a large bowl; beat at medium speed of an electric mixer until blended. Add egg substitute and vanilla, beating well. Combine all-purpose flour and next 3 ingredients; add to creamed mixture, and beat 1 minute. Stir in oats and raisins.

Drop dough by teaspoonfuls onto baking sheets coated with cooking spray. Flatten dough with a fork. Combine 1 tablespoon sugar and cinnamon; sprinkle over cookies. Bake at 350° for 12 minutes. Remove from baking sheets; let cool on wire racks.
Yield: 30 cookies (serving size: 2 cookies).

Per serving: Calories 113 (27% from fat)
Fat 3g (Sat 1g   Mono 2g   Poly 1g)
Protein 2g   Carbohydrate 19g   Fiber 1g
Cholesterol 0mg   Sodium 124mg

ORANGE-GLAZED OATMEAL COOKIES

Count 1 serving as:
1½ Starch

½ cup mixed dried fruit, finely chopped
3 tablespoons fresh orange juice
⅓ cup sugar
⅓ cup unsweetened applesauce
¼ cup light-colored corn syrup
¼ cup fat-free egg substitute
1 tablespoon grated orange rind, divided
1½ cups regular oats, uncooked
¾ cup all-purpose flour
¼ cup whole wheat flour
1 teaspoon baking soda
Vegetable cooking spray
½ cup sifted powdered sugar
2 teaspoons fresh orange juice

Combine chopped fruit and 3 tablespoons juice in a large bowl; let stand 30 minutes. Add ⅓ cup sugar, next 3 ingredients, and 2 teaspoons orange rind, stirring well. Combine oats and next 3 ingredients; add to fruit mixture, stirring well.

Drop dough by level tablespoonfuls onto baking sheets coated with cooking spray. Bake at 350° for 9 minutes. Remove cookies from baking sheets, and let cool on wire racks.

Combine powdered sugar, 2 teaspoons orange juice, and remaining 1 teaspoon orange rind, stirring with a wire whisk until smooth. Spread glaze evenly over cookies.
Yield: 3 dozen (serving size: 2 cookies).

Per serving: Calories 104 (5% from fat)
Fat 1g (Sat tr Mono tr Poly tr)
Protein 2g Carbohydrate 24g Fiber 1g
Cholesterol 0mg Sodium 80mg

PUMPKIN-DATE COOKIES

Count 1 serving as:
1 Starch

½ cup firmly packed brown sugar
¼ cup sugar
¼ cup margarine, softened
1 cup canned pumpkin
1 teaspoon vanilla extract
1 egg
1½ cups all-purpose flour
1½ cups wheat bran cereal (such as Bran Flakes)
¼ cup nutlike cereal nuggets (such as Grape-Nuts)
½ teaspoon baking soda
¼ cup chopped dates
Vegetable cooking spray

Combine first 3 ingredients in a large bowl; beat at medium speed of an electric mixer until light in color. Add pumpkin, vanilla, and egg, beating well. Combine flour and next 3 ingredients; gradually add to creamed mixture, beating well. Stir in dates. Cover and chill dough 30 minutes.

Drop dough by rounded teaspoonfuls onto baking sheets coated with cooking spray. Bake at 375° for 12 minutes or until firm to the touch and lightly browned on edges. Remove cookies from baking sheets, and let cool on wire racks.
Yield: 5 dozen (serving size: 2 cookies).

Per serving: Calories 76 (21% from fat)
Fat 2g (Sat tr Mono 1g Poly 1g)
Protein 1g Carbohydrate 14g Fiber 1g
Cholesterol 6mg Sodium 67mg

PEANUT-BUTTERY PUFFS

Count 1 serving as:
2 Starch
1 Fat

¼ cup plus 1 tablespoon chunky
   nonhydrogenated peanut butter, divided
¼ cup cooked bulgur wheat with soy grits
   (cooked without salt or fat)
¼ cup firmly packed brown sugar
1 tablespoon water
1 package active dry yeast
¼ cup warm water (105° to 115°)
¾ cup warm skim milk (105° to 115°)
¾ cup fat-free egg substitute
2 tablespoons sugar
1 tablespoon vegetable oil
½ teaspoon salt
1½ cups all-purpose flour
1½ cups whole wheat flour
Vegetable cooking spray
½ cup sifted powdered sugar
1 tablespoon skim milk
½ teaspoon vanilla extract

Combine ¼ cup peanut butter and next 3
ingredients in a medium bowl, and set aside.

Combine yeast and warm water in a 1-cup
liquid measuring cup; let stand 5 minutes.
Combine yeast mixture, ¾ cup milk, and next
4 ingredients. Combine flours, and gradually
add to yeast mixture to form a soft dough.

Divide dough into 24 equal portions. Place 1
portion in each of 12 muffin cups coated with
cooking spray, and flatten. Top each with 1
teaspoon peanut butter mixture. Top with 12
remaining portions of dough, spreading to
cover filling. Let rise in a warm place (85°),
free from drafts, 45 minutes to 1 hour or until
doubled in bulk. Bake at 350° for 20 to 25
minutes or until lightly browned.

Combine powdered sugar, 1 tablespoon
skim milk, vanilla, and remaining 1 tablespoon peanut butter, stirring well. Spread
sugar mixture on warm rolls.
Yield: 1 dozen (serving size: 1 roll).

Per serving: Calories 216 (21% from fat)
Fat 5g (Sat 1g   Mono 2g   Poly 1g)
Protein 7g   Carbohydrate 37g   Fiber 3g
Cholesterol tr   Sodium 147mg

RECIPE INDEX

Almonds
Crêpes, Almond-Chicken, 84
Salad Stuffed Tomatoes, Chicken, 86
Appetizers
Canapés, Salmon, 30
Cauliflower Nuggets, 29
Dips
Chick-Pea Dip, 28
Salsa, Black Bean, 28
Salsa, Fresh Tomato, 29
Mix, Crunchy Snack, 30
Apples
Betty, Lemon-Glazed Apple, 131
Cobbler, Apple, 132
Ginger-Yogurt Dressing, Fresh Fruit with, 101
Muffins, Apple-Nut, 34
Applesauce
Baked Tropical Fruit, 129
Bread, Apricot-Walnut, 36
Cake, Lemon, 134
Cake, Whole Wheat Carrot, 133
Cookies, Carrot, 135
Cookies, Oatmeal Raisin, 135
Cookies, Orange-Glazed Oatmeal, 136
Loaf, Citrus, 134
Muffins, Apple-Nut, 34
Apricot-Walnut Bread, 36
Artichoke-Tomato Sauce, Pasta with, 67
Asparagus
Skillet Rice and Chicken, 90

Bananas
Baked Tropical Fruit, 129
Bread, Banana-Nut, 36
Ice Cream, Banana, 126
Barbecue
Chicken, Barbecued, 93
Steak, Barbecued Round, 77
Barley
Hearty Barley, 65
Stuffed Yellow Squash, Vegetable-, 122
Beans
Baked Navy Beans and Corn, 58
Barley, Hearty, 65
Black Bean Patties with Fresh Tomato
Salsa, 60
Black Bean Pie, 60
Black Bean Salsa, 28
Bulgur, Mexican, 51
Casserole, Rice and Bean, 58
Chili, Vegetarian, 113
Dip, Chick-Pea, 28
Green Beans, Italian-Style, 116
Pinto Bean and Cornbread Bake, 61

Red Beans with Ham, 80
Salads
Green Bean Salad, Marinated, 102
Mexican Salad, 61
Soup, Black Bean-Butternut Squash, 112
Soup, Navy Bean, 113
Soup, Vegetable Beef, 114
Soup, Vegetarian Vegetable, 111
Tostadas, Spicy Vegetarian, 62
Beef
Sandwiches, Roast Beef, 78
Soup, Vegetable Beef, 114
Steaks
Filet Mignon, Marinated, 78
Round Steak, Barbecued, 77
Sirloin, Swiss-Style, 77
Stir-Fry, Beef and Broccoli, 76
Beef, Ground
Meatballs and Vegetables, 75
Meat Loaf, Savory 75
Peppers, Stuffed Green, 72
Biscuits
Crispy Biscuits, 32
Onion Drop Biscuits, Savory, 32
Blueberries
Bread, Blueberry, 39
Salad, Blueberry-Melon, 100
Breads. See also specific types.
Apricot-Walnut Bread, 36
Banana-Nut Bread, 36
Blueberry Bread, 39
Honey-Wheat Bread, 39
Toast, Parmesan, 35
Broccoli
Barley, Hearty, 65
Pasta Primavera, 68
Pizza, Garden, 69
Potatoes, Veggie-Topped Baked, 70
Quiche, Chicken, 85
Salad, Creamy Broccoli, 102
Salad, Italian Broccoli-Cauliflower, 103
Soup, Cheesy Potato-Broccoli, 108
Stir-Fry, Beef and Broccoli, 76
Bulgur
Mexican Bulgur, 51
Peanut-Buttery Puffs, 137
Peppers, Stuffed Green, 72
Burritos, Breakfast, 62

Cakes. See also Breads, Cookies.
Carrot Cake, Whole Wheat, 133
Citrus Loaf, 134
Lemon Cake, 134
Pound Cake, Chocolate, 132

Cantaloupe. *See* Melons.
Carrots
    Cake, Whole Wheat Carrot, 133
    Casserole, Summer Squash, 123
    Cookies, Carrot, 135
    Lasagna, Florentine, 66
    Medley on Orzo, Vegetable, 65
    Minted Carrots, 116
    Pasta Primavera, 68
    Roasted Potatoes and Carrots, 119
    Soup, Cheesy Potato-Broccoli, 108
    Soup, Lentil, 108
    Soup, Vegetable Beef, 114
    Soup, Vegetarian Vegetable, 111
Casseroles
    Chicken and Rice Casserole, 89
    Corn Casseroles, Mexican, 64
    Rice and Bean Casserole, 58
    Vegetable
        Mushroom-Spinach Casserole, 64
        Squash Casserole, Summer, 123
        Sweet Potato Casserole, 120
Cauliflower
    Medley, Cajun Cauliflower, 117
    Nuggets, Cauliflower, 29
    Salad, Cauliflower and Green Pea, 103
    Salad, Creamy Broccoli, 102
    Salad, Italian Broccoli-Cauliflower, 103
    Salad, Zesty Cauliflower, 104
Celery
    Salad, Cauliflower and Green Pea, 103
    Salad, Curried Chicken, 85
    Salad Stuffed Tomatoes, Chicken, 86
    Soup, Vegetable Beef, 114
    Soup, Vegetarian Vegetable, 111
Cheese
    Baked Tomatoes with Spinach, 123
    Breads
        Cornbread, Jalapeño, 33
        Rolls, Cream Cheese-Chive, 40
        Toast, Parmesan, 35
    Burritos, Breakfast, 62
    Casseroles
        Corn Casseroles, Mexican, 64
        Mushroom-Spinach Casserole, 64
        Rice and Bean Casserole, 58
    Crêpes, Orange, 130
    Fettuccine, Parmesan, 54
    Frosting, Cream Cheese, 133
    Lasagna, Florentine, 66
    Macaroni and Cheese, 63
    Pasta Primavera, 68
    Pie, Black Bean, 60
    Pie, Turkey-Chili, 97
    Pizza, Garden, 69
    Pizza, Mushroom-Onion, 70

Quiche, Chicken, 85
    Salad, Mexican, 61
    Soup, Cheesy Potato-Broccoli, 108
    Spaghetti Squares, Italian, 68
    Topping, Baked Potatoes with Cream
      Cheese, 119
    Tostadas, Spicy Vegetarian, 62
    Turkey Cutlets Italiano, 98
    Vegetables
        Eggplant Parmesan Pasta, 67
        Peppers, Stuffed Green, 72
        Tomatoes with Spinach, Baked, 123
        Zucchini, Baked Greek, 124
Chicken
    Barbecued Chicken, 93
    Cashew Chicken, 88
    Casserole, Chicken and Rice, 89
    Crêpes, Almond-Chicken, 84
    Hawaiian Chicken, 94
    Kabobs, Chicken, 86
    Lemon-Pepper, Chicken, 94
    Pasta Primavera, Chicken, 93
    Polenta, Mexican Chicken on, 87
    Quiche, Chicken, 85
    Raspberry Chicken with Brown Rice, 95
    Rosemary-Ginger Chicken, 95
    Salads
        Curried Chicken Salad, 85
        Tomatoes, Chicken Salad Stuffed, 86
    Skillet Rice and Chicken, 90
    Soup, Chicken-Noodle, 114
    Supreme, Chicken, 96
Chili
    Pie, Turkey-Chili, 97
    Vegetarian Chili, 113
Chocolate Pound Cake, 132
Cookies
    Carrot Cookies, 135
    Oatmeal Cookies, Orange-Glazed, 136
    Oatmeal Raisin Cookies, 135
    Pumpkin-Date Cookies, 136
Corn
    Baked Navy Beans and Corn, 58
    Bake, Pinto Bean and Cornbread, 61
    Casseroles, Mexican Corn, 64
    Curried Corn, 117
    Pie, Turkey-Chili, 97
    Salad, Marinated Green Bean, 102
    Salad, Mexican, 61
    Soup, Vegetable Beef, 114
    Tostadas, Spicy Vegetarian, 62
Cornbreads
    Bake, Pinto Bean and Cornbread, 61
    Golden Cornbread, 33
    Jalapeño Cornbread, 33
Couscous Salad, Chilled, 50

Cranberry-Orange Muffins, 34
Crêpes
    Almond-Chicken Crêpes, 84
    Orange Crêpes, 130
Cucumbers
    Dressing, Cucumber Salad, 106
    Salad, Curried Shrimp and Pasta, 48
Curry
    Corn, Curried, 117
    Lamb, Curried, 80
    Pasta Salad, Curried Shrimp and, 48
    Potatoes and Peppers, Curried, 118
    Rice, Curried, 51
    Salad, Curried Chicken, 85

Date Cookies, Pumpkin-, 136
Desserts. *See also* specific types.
    Apple Betty, Lemon-Glazed, 131
    Baked Tropical Fruit, 129
Dressings. *See* Salad Dressings.

Eggplant
    Medley on Orzo, Vegetable, 65
    Pasta, Eggplant Parmesan, 67

Fettuccine, Parmesan, 54
Fish. *See also* specific types and Seafood.
    Catfish Gumbo, 42
    Flounder, Vegetable-Topped, 42
    Grouper Sandwiches, 43
    Mahimahi, Lemon-Grilled, 43
    Orange Roughy, Oven-Fried, 44
    Snapper, Greek-Style, 45
    Sole, Baked, 45
    Swordfish, Sweet-and-Sour, 46
French Toast with Strawberries, 63
Frosting, Cream Cheese, 133
Fruit. *See also* specific types.
    Baked Tropical Fruit, 129
    Ginger-Yogurt Dressing, Fresh Fruit with, 101
    Medley, Poached Fruit, 129
    Salad with Orange-Yogurt Dressing, Fruit, 101

Grapes
    Medley, Poached Fruit, 129
    Salad with Orange-Yogurt Dressing, Fruit, 101
Gumbo, Catfish, 42

Ham, Red Beans with, 80
Honey
    Bread, Honey-Wheat, 39
    Cake, Whole Wheat Carrot, 133
    Dressing, Pineapple-Honey Mustard, 106
    Muffins, Glazed Lemon-Yogurt, 35
    Salad, Spicy Melon, 100
Honeydew. *See* Melons.

Ice Creams and Sherbets
    Banana Ice Cream, 126

Kabobs
    Chicken Kabobs, 86

Lamb, Curried, 80
Lasagna, Florentine, 66
Lemon
    Apple Betty, Lemon-Glazed, 131
    Cake, Lemon, 134
    Chicken, Lemon-Pepper, 94
    Mahimahi, Lemon-Grilled, 43
    Muffins, Glazed Lemon-Yogurt, 35
    Spinach, Lemon-Pepper, 121
Lentils
    Soup, Lentil, 108
Lime
    Loaf, Citrus, 134
    Medley, Poached Fruit, 129
    Salad, Spicy Melon, 100
Linguine
    Marinara Sauce, Linguine with, 54

Macaroni
    Cheese, Macaroni and, 63
    Soup, Vegetarian Vegetable, 111
Mangoes
    Baked Tropical Fruit, 129
    Salsa, Pork Tenderloin with Mango, 82
Meatballs and Vegetables, 75
Meat Loaf. *See* Beef, Ground/Meat Loaf.
Melons
    Barley, Hearty, 65
    Fruit with Ginger-Yogurt Dressing, Fresh, 101
    Salad, Blueberry-Melon, 100
    Salad, Spicy Melon, 100
Muffins
    Apple-Nut Muffins, 34
    Cranberry-Orange Muffins, 34
    Lemon-Yogurt Muffins, Glazed, 35
Mushrooms
    Casserole, Mushroom-Spinach, 64
    Chicken Supreme, 96
    Kabobs, Chicken, 86
    Lasagna, Florentine, 66
    Meatballs and Vegetables, 75
    Medley, Cajun Cauliflower, 117
    Medley on Orzo, Vegetable, 65
    Pizza, Mushroom-Onion, 70
    Soup, Wild Rice, 111
    Spaghetti Squares, Italian, 68
    Stroganoff, Turkey, 98
    Stuffed Yellow Squash, Vegetable-, 122
Mustard Dressing, Pineapple-Honey, 106

Noodles
  Pasta with Artichoke Tomato Sauce, 67
  Soup, Chicken-Noodle, 114
  Stroganoff, Turkey, 98

Oatmeal
  Bread, Apricot-Walnut, 36
  Cookies, Oatmeal Raisin, 135
  Cookies, Orange-Glazed Oatmeal, 136
Olives
  Salad, Greek Potato, 105
  Skillet Rice and Chicken, 90
Onions
  Beans, Italian-Style Green, 116
  Biscuits, Savory Onion Drop, 32
  Casserole, Summer Squash, 123
  Curried Potatoes and Peppers, 118
  Pizza, Mushroom-Onion, 70
  Potatoes with Green Onions, 118
  Salad, Italian Broccoli-Cauliflower, 103
  Soup, Lentil, 108
Oranges
  Chicken, Cashew, 88
  Chicken, Hawaiian, 94
  Crêpes, Almond-Chicken, 84
  Desserts
      Cookies, Orange-Glazed Oatmeal, 136
      Crêpes, Orange, 130
  Loaf, Citrus, 134
  Muffins, Cranberry-Orange, 34
  Rice, Curried, 51
  Salad with Orange-Yogurt Dressing, Fruit, 101
Orzo
  Chilled Orzo, Zesty, 57
  Medley on Orzo, Vegetable, 65

Pastas. See also specific types.
  Artichoke-Tomato Sauce, Pasta with, 67
  Eggplant Parmesan Pasta, 67
  Primavera, Chicken Pasta, 93
  Primavera, Pasta, 68
  Salad, Curried Shrimp and Pasta, 48
Peaches
  Baked Tropical Fruit, 129
  Medley, Poached Fruit, 129
Peanut Butter
  Kabobs, Chicken, 86
  Puffs, Peanut-Buttery, 137
Peas
  Black-Eyed Peas and Rice, 57
  Salad, Cauliflower and Green Pea, 103
  Salad, Dilled Potato and Pea, 105
  Skillet Rice and Chicken, 90
Pecans
  Apple Betty, Lemon-Glazed, 131
  Bread, Banana-Nut, 36

Cake, Whole Wheat Carrot, 133
Casserole, Sweet Potato, 120
Salad, Creamy Broccoli, 102
Peppers
  Chicken, Cashew, 88
  Cornbread, Jalapeño, 33
  Curried Potatoes and Peppers, 118
  Salad, Marinated Green Bean, 102
  Salad, Tangy Zucchini, 104
  Salad, Zesty Cauliflower, 104
  Spaghetti, Tangy Turkey, 96
  Stuffed Green Peppers, 72
  Sweet-and-Sour Swordfish, 46
Pies and Pastries
  Cobbler, Apple, 132
  Grasshopper Pie, 126
  Main Dish
      Black Bean Pie, 60
      Turkey-Chili Pie, 97
  Pastries and Crusts
      Rice Crust, 97
Pineapple
  Baked Tropical Fruit, 129
  Barley, Hearty, 65
  Casserole, Sweet Potato, 120
  Chicken, Hawaiian, 94
  Dressing, Pineapple-Honey Mustard, 106
  Salad, Curried Shrimp and Pasta, 48
  Salad, Tuna on Bagels, 47
  Salad with Orange-Yogurt Dressing, Fruit, 101
  Sweet-and-Sour Pork, 81
  Sweet-and-Sour Swordfish, 46
Pizza
  Garden Pizza, 69
  Mushroom-Onion Pizza, 70
Polenta, Mexican Chicken on, 87
Pork. See also Ham.
  Loin, Roasted Pork, 82
  Sweet-and-Sour Pork, 81
  Tenderloin with Mango Salsa, Pork, 82
Potatoes
  Baked
      Cream Cheese Topping, Baked Potatoes
        with, 119
      Veggie-Topped Baked Potatoes, 70
  Curried Potatoes and Peppers, 118
  Green Onions, Potatoes with, 118
  Mashed Potatoes, Horseradish, 120
  Pie, Black Bean, 60
  Roasted Potatoes and Carrots, 119
  Salad, Dilled Potato and Pea, 105
  Salad, Greek Potato, 105
  Soup, Cheesy Potato-Broccoli, 108
  Soup, Vegetable Beef, 114
Potatoes, Sweet
  Casserole, Sweet Potato, 120

Pudding, Rice, 131
Pumpkin-Date Cookies, 136

Quiches
  Chicken Quiche, 85

Raisins
  Cookies, Oatmeal Raisin, 135
  Pudding, Rice, 131
  Salad, Creamy Broccoli, 102
  Salad, Curried Chicken, 85
Raspberries
  Chicken with Brown Rice, Raspberry, 95
  Medley, Poached Fruit, 129
Rice
  Black-Eyed Peas and Rice, 57
  Brown Rice, Gingered, 52
  Brown Rice, Raspberry Chicken with, 95
  Brown Rice, Savory, 53
  Casserole, Chicken and Rice, 89
  Casserole, Rice and Bean, 58
  Crust, Rice, 97
  Curried Rice, 51
  Fiesta Rice, 52
  Pork, Sweet-and-Sour, 81
  Pudding, Rice, 131
  Skillet Rice and Chicken, 90
  Stir-Fry, Beef and Broccoli, 76
  Wild Rice Soup, 111
  Yellow and Brown Rice, 53
Rolls and Buns. See also Breads.
  Cream Cheese-Chive Rolls, 40
  Peanut-Buttery Puffs, 137

Salad Dressings
  Cucumber Salad Dressing, 106
  Ginger-Yogurt Dressing, Fresh Fruit with, 101
  Orange-Yogurt Dressing, Fruit Salad with, 101
  Pineapple-Honey Mustard Dressing, 106
  Yogurt Dressing, 50
Salads
  Chicken
      Curried Chicken Salad, 85
      Stuffed Tomatoes, Chicken Salad, 86
  Couscous Salad, Chilled, 50
  Green Bean Salad, Marinated, 102
  Fruit
      Blueberry-Melon Salad, 100
      Ginger-Yogurt Dressing, Fresh
        Fruit with, 101
      Melon Salad, Spicy, 100
      Orange-Yogurt Dressing, Fruit
        Salad with, 101
  Mexican Salad, 61
  Potato and Pea Salad, Dilled, 105
  Potato Salad, Greek, 105

Shrimp and Pasta Salad, Curried, 48
  Tuna Salad on Bagels, 47
  Vegetable
      Broccoli-Cauliflower Salad, Italian, 103
      Broccoli Salad, Creamy, 102
      Cauliflower and Green Pea Salad, 103
      Cauliflower Salad, Zesty, 104
      Zucchini Salad, Tangy, 104
Salmon
  Baked Salmon, Zesty, 44
  Canapés, Salmon, 30
Sandwiches
  Grouper Sandwiches, 43
  Roast Beef Sandwiches, 78
Sauces
  Artichoke-Tomato Sauce, Pasta with, 67
  Marinara Sauce, Linguine with, 54
  Salsa, Black Bean, 28
  Salsa, Fresh Tomato, 29
  Salsa, Pork Tenderloin with Mango, 82
Seafood. See also specific types and Fish.
  Sautéed Seafood, Garlic, 47
Shrimp and Pasta Salad, Curried, 48
Soups. See also Chili, Gumbos.
  Bean-Butternut Squash Soup, Black, 112
  Bean Soup, Navy, 113
  Chicken-Noodle Soup, 114
  Lentil Soup, 108
  Potato-Broccoli Soup, Cheesy, 108
  Rice Soup, Wild, 111
  Vegetable Beef Soup, 114
  Vegetable Soup, Vegetarian, 111
  Zucchini Soup, 112
Spaghetti
  Eggplant Parmesan Pasta, 67
  Squares, Italian Spaghetti, 68
  Tetrazzini, Veal, 79
  Turkey Spaghetti, Tangy, 96
Spinach
  Baked Tomatoes with Spinach, 123
  Casserole, Mushroom-Spinach, 64
  Lasagna, Florentine, 66
  Lemon-Pepper Spinach, 121
Squash. See also Zucchini.
  Butternut Squash Soup, Black Bean-, 112
  Spanish Squash, 121
  Yellow
      Baked Potatoes, Veggie-Topped, 70
      Casserole, Summer Squash, 123
      Flounder, Vegetable-Topped, 42
      Pizza, Garden, 69
      Stuffed Yellow Squash, Vegetable-, 122
Strawberries
  French Toast with Strawberries, 63
  Fruit Salad with Orange-Yogurt Dressing, 101
  Fruit with Ginger-Yogurt Dressing, Fresh, 101

Stroganoff
  Turkey Stroganoff, 98
Sweet-and-Sour
  Pork, Sweet-and-Sour, 81
  Swordfish, Sweet-and-Sour, 46

Tomatoes
  Baked Tomatoes with Spinach, 123
  Bake, Pinto Beans and Cornbread, 61
  Beans, Italian-Style Green, 116
  Bulgur, Mexican, 51
  Chili, Vegetarian, 113
  Flounder, Vegetable-Topped, 42
  Kabobs, Chicken, 86
  Medley, Cajun Cauliflower, 117
  Salad, Chilled Couscous, 50
  Salad, Mexican, 61
  Salsa, Black Bean Patties with Fresh
    Tomato, 60
  Salsa, Fresh Tomato, 29
  Sauce, Linguine with Marinara, 54
  Sauce, Pasta with Artichoke-Tomato, 67
  Soup, Vegetarian Vegetable, 111
  Spaghetti Squares, Italian, 68
  Spaghetti, Tangy Turkey, 96
  Squash, Spanish, 121
  Stuffed Tomatoes, Chicken Salad, 86
  Tostadas, Spicy Vegetarian, 62
Tortillas. See also Burritos.
  Tostadas, Spicy Vegetarian, 62
Tuna
  Salad on Bagels, Tuna, 47
Turkey
  Cutlets Italiano, Turkey, 98
  Meat Loaf, Savory, 75
  Pie, Turkey-Chili, 97
  Spaghetti, Tangy Turkey, 96
  Stroganoff, Turkey, 98

Veal
  Tetrazzini, Veal, 79
Vegetables. See also specific types.
  Chili, Vegetarian, 113
  Flounder, Vegetable-Topped, 42
  Meatballs and Vegetables, 75
  Medley on Orzo, Vegetable, 65
  Nuggets, Cauliflower, 29
  Pizza, Garden, 69
  Primavera, Pasta, 68
  Pork Loin, Roasted, 82
  Potatoes, Veggie-Topped Baked, 70
  Soups
      Beef Soup, Vegetable, 114
      Vegetarian Vegetable Soup, 111
  Squash, Vegetable-Stuffed Yellow, 122
  Tostadas, Spicy Vegetarian, 62

Walnuts
  Bread, Apricot-Walnut, 36
  Muffins, Apple-Nut, 34
Wild Rice. See Rice/Wild Rice.

Yogurt
  Apple Betty, Lemon-Glazed, 131
  Biscuits, Crispy, 32
  Chicken, Lemon-Pepper, 94
  Cornbread, Golden, 33
  Crêpes, Almond-Chicken, 84
  Dressing, Fresh Fruit with Ginger-Yogurt, 101
  Dressing, Fruit Salad with Orange-Yogurt, 101
  Dressing, Yogurt, 50
  Loaf, Citrus, 134
  Muffins, Glazed Lemon-Yogurt, 35
  Pasta Primavera, 68
  Tostadas, Spicy Vegetarian, 62
  Salad, Curried Shrimp and Pasta, 48

Zucchini
  Baked Greek Zucchini, 124
  Chili, Vegetarian, 113
  Flounder, Vegetable-Topped, 42
  Medley, Cajun Cauliflower, 117
  Medley on Orzo, Vegetable, 65
  Salad, Tangy Zucchini, 104
  Soup, Zucchini, 112

Subject Index

Alcohol, 18
American Heart Association, dietary
    recommendations, 12, 14, 18
Anemia, iron-deficiency, 18
Antioxidants, 16, 17

Blood pressure, 8
Body Mass Index (BMI), 9, 10
Breastfeeding, 18

Calcium, 15, 16, 17
Calories, 18, 23
Carotenoids, 17
Cholesterol, 7, 10, 13, 21
Cooking, low-fat techniques, 26

Diabetes, 18
Diastolic blood pressure, 8
Dietary Guidelines, American Heart
    Association, 18

EatRight Food Groups, 22, 23, 24, 25
Eggs, 26
Exercise. *See* Physical Activity.

Fat
    American Heart Association
        recommendations for, 12, 18
    heart disease risk and, 7, 12
    monounsaturated, 12
    polyunsaturated, 12
    saturated, 12
    servings of, 22, 23, 24, 25
    trans, 13
Fiber, 11, 15, 21
Fluids, 26
Folate, 16, 17
Folic acid. *See* Folate.
Fruits
    increasing intake of, 7, 18, 22
    servings of, 22, 23, 24, 25

Heart disease
    diet and, 7, 11
    Heart Risk Quiz, 10
    high blood pressure and, 8, 12
    lifestyle changes and, 7
    physical activity and, 7, 8
    risk factors, 7, 8
    weight and, 7, 9

Labels, 14, 15

Magnesium, 16, 17
Meat/Dairy, servings of, 22, 23, 24, 25
Meats, low-fat preparation of, 26

Occasional foods, 22

Physical activity, 7, 8
Phytochemicals, 17
Portion sizes, 26
Potassium, 16, 17
Preferred foods, 22, 24, 25

Recommended Daily Allowance
    (RDA), 15, 16, 17, 21

Salt. *See* Sodium.
Serving sizes, 24, 25, 26
Servings per day, 22, 23
Sodium, 7, 12, 14, 18, 21
Soluble fiber, 11
Special Occasion foods, 22, 23, 24, 25
Starches, servings of, 22, 23, 24, 25
Systolic blood pressure, 8, 10

Vegetables
    heart-smart choices, 11
    increasing intake of, 7, 18, 22
    servings of, 23, 24, 25
Vitamin C, 15, 16, 17
Vitamin E, 16, 17
Vitamin supplements, 18

Water, intake of, 26
Weight, 9, 10, 18, 23

Fabrics in your kit
may be different.

Stencil Sheets
Trace onto paper or fabric.

Stickers
Decorate posters, pictures, and other craft projects.

Fabric Scraps
Add to your accessories or clothes.

Yarn
Use the 2 ft. (61 cm) yarn to decorate your clothes and room decor.

Washi Tape
Use for any awesome project you want.

Patterned Paper
The papers can be used for any room decor or party decorating project.

NAIL POLISH

SUPPLIES

MAKE-UP

NECKLACES

HAIR STUFF

WASHI TAPE

ART SCRAPS

So Awesome!

I Love this!

Looks Nice!

So cute!

Gotta have!

I made it!

#SoPhotoSilly

#ThisIsMe!

#NomNomNom

#GottaHaveIt

#TotallyAwesome

#TheBestEver

The beauty of making something your own is that there are a lot of materials out there, within your own home, recycled material, and even from nature. Use what you find to create great looks that are cheap and trendy!

Look for these:

- Aluminum foil
- Newspaper
- Wrapping paper
- Cookie cutters: When you aren't baking, these act as great stencils!
- Mod Podge or fabric glue

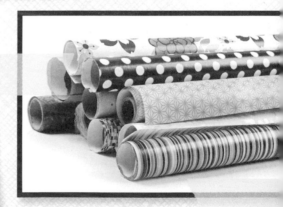

#Imadethis!

5

FASHION

Goal's

⭐Squeals⭐

Lookin'
FAB
TODAY!

▶ YOUR STYLE IS
UNIQUE,
even if you don't know it.

To develop your fabulous style, try glamming up some of your humdrum outfits and accessories. Some fun organization tips will keep these projects moving along.

Warning!
Gotta get permission from the 'rents before glamming up your clothes!

#accessories

#shopping *soAwesome

TIPS AND CRAFTS IN THIS SECTION:

Pages 8-11: All about clothes and what looks good on you

12-13: #instaAwesomeTips to keep your fave outfits organized

14-15: Decorate your hangers (Glamorize your closet!)

16-17: Accessorize your wardrobe (More like obsessorize!)

18-19: Make a jewelry holder

20-23: Decorate your kicks

Brainstorm a few hashtags that

\#

\#

\#

\#

\#

\#

\#

\#

✓ Things to think about:

Check off the ones that inspire your fashion style.

[ ] Viral video stars

[ ] TV and movie celebs/athletes

[ ] Different decades (go retro!)

[ ] Different countries

[ ] Your friends

[ ] Favorite colors and patterns

[ ] The weather

[ ] The seasons

[ ] Comfort

Don't forget to take pictures along the way! #instaAwesomeStyle

7

All About Clothes and
WHAT LOOKS GOOD ON YOU

Your clothes have the power to tell the world who you are. But with all the clothes hitting the racks, how can you REALLY know which outfits look best on you? #selfie

Here are some tips to help you be a

#SelfieRockstar!

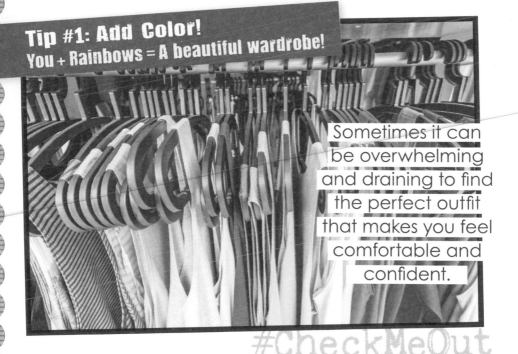

Tip #1: Add Color!
You + Rainbows = A beautiful wardrobe!

Sometimes it can be overwhelming and draining to find the perfect outfit that makes you feel comfortable and confident.

#CheckMeOut

Blacks, whites, and grays are the perfect basics for your wardrobe, but adding colors will help you get noticed! Let's see what colors look best against your skin tone—it's time for an #experiGLAM!

#EXPERIGLAM = A FASHION, STYLE, AND BEAUTY EXPERIMENT

#Stunning

TRY IT!

1. Take pieces of clothing out of your closet or dresser, each a different color of the rainbow.

2. Hold up each piece of clothing to your face, one piece at a time.

3. Take a selfie of each item by your face.

4. Compare the selfies to see which colors YOU think look best.

Always include your favorite color in your wardrobe. If you like what you're wearing, you'll smile more often.

Put on the
★ COOLEST OUTFIT EVER ★

Here are some fun and flirty color combinations that look great together:

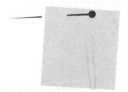

yellow and gray

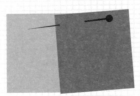

orange and hot pink

A smile is the BEST accessory a girl like you can wear.

purple and brown

turquoise and red

navy blue and apple green

Tip #2: Watch out for pattern clash chaos!

Your pieces should POP!

Fun accessories make a plain wardrobe pop. Try a couple of different colored bags for some pizzazz.

Don't put too many different patterns and fabrics together. If you have too many types of fabrics and patterns, nothing stands out, including you.

Tip #3: Size matters!

MAKE SURE YOU GET A SIZE THAT IS JUST RIGHT FOR YOU. Remember that cotton shrinks. If something seems a bit small when you try it on, get the next size up. It will shrink a bit. You'll feel comfortable and confident throughout the day when you wear clothes that are a perfect fit for you.

#Flawless

10 1 2 3 4 5 6 7 8 9 10

Here are some classic pieces to get you started:

Tip #4: Collect basics

Jeans

Black T

COLLECT THE STAPLE PIECES

that easily mix and match with everything else in your wardrobe.

Cardigan

Tank tops

Black skirt

There is no need to scour your closet for hours.

Tip #5: No Fashion Worries!

BUY THE CLOTHES THAT FEEL GOOD AND LOOK GOOD ON YOU. The worst feeling in the world is wearing an outfit that doesn't feel right!

Here's the trick — if you buy what you want to wear, staying true to you, you're going to be much happier and feel confident throughout the day, instead of squirming in your seat.

1

#INSTAAWESOMETIPS TO KEEP YOUR FAVE OUTFITS ORGANIZED

When taking your outfit selfies, use props or accessories that go well with the outfit. Or have a fashion selfie party with your friends!

STAY ORGANIZED TO HELP YOU GET READY FASTER IN THE MORNING!

And who doesn't love an extra bit of snooze time? Use a few of these tips to remind yourself of your fave outfits!

#INSTATIP: *Take selfies in your favorite outfits.*

Print these photos and place them around your closet door or your dresser to remember your favorite combinations. You'll make fast decisions in the morning, giving you more time to focus on other things – like your hair, accessories, makeup, catching up with a friend via video call, or just a moment to chill.

Share your outfit selfies with friends. Text a few options to friends and have them vote for which outfit you should wear! But remember, wear what you feel best in!

If you can't print the pictures, organize them in your phone or computer so the images are at your fingertips.

#INSTATIP:

Organize your closet or drawers with any of these ideas.

1) type — pants, tanks, cardigans, dresses, long sleeve, short sleeve

2) color

3) favorite outfits

#INSTATIP:

Color coordinate your hangers to reflect certain types of outfits: dressy, sporty, chill, lazy, or favorites.

#INSTATIP:

Make a chart and tape it on the outside of your closet to remind you which hanger color means what.

#INSTATIP:

While organizing, think of outfits that match your phone case, match your friends, or are inspired by your favorite celebs.

★Love★

DECORATE
YOUR HANGERS

You've seen how organizing your wardrobe can help save time and fashion headaches. Decorate some hangers to make your closet fun!

make it!

WHAT YOU'LL NEED:

[ ] wooden or plastic hangers

[ ] washi tape, tissue paper, fabric, ribbon, or yarn

WHAT TO DO:

1 Lay out some newspaper on your work surface.

2 Add glue to one side of the hanger.

3 Cover the entire hanger with wrapping paper, tissue paper, or fabric.

4 Let dry for a few hours.

5 Repeat steps 2–4 for the other side of the hanger.

6 Repeat for all of your hangers.

Here are some other
HANGER DECORATING OPTIONS

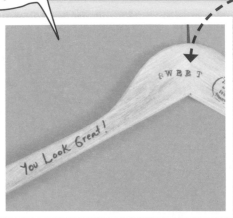

Use a rubber stamp or permanent marker to add words and phrases to your hangers. Be sure to let this dry overnight, or it could stain your clothes.

#instaTip:
Do several hangers at a time.

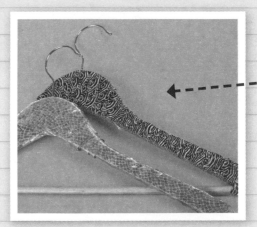

Cover the upper part of your hanger with washi tape, duct tape, yarn, or ribbon.

soAwesome

Accessorize
YOUR WARDROBE

Are you obsessed with accessories?
They should be called #obsessories, right? Here are a few ways that you can make your obsessories yours!

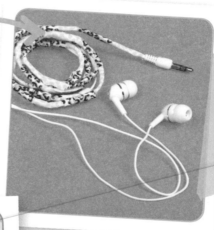

Earbuds and Charger cords

1 Wrap different-colored string, thread, yarn, or washi tape around the earbuds and cord.

Sunglasses

1 Use Mod Podge or glue to adhere jewels, beads, buttons, or studs to your sunglasses.

2 Cover the sides in washi tape.

3 Cut washi tape into strips and paint nail polish between strips. Take off the tape.

#Obsessories

Headbands

1 Cover a plain plastic headband with washi tape, fabric, ribbon, or yarn.

2 Use glue to embellish with studs, bows, jewels, pearls, flowers, or sequins.

#instaTip:
If you don't have glue available, clear nail polish will also do the trick.

Washi tape or fabric jewelry

1 Cut washi tape into your desired shape.

2 Put thread in the middle on the sticky side and tape the same shape lined up with the other.

3 Do this for earrings or bracelets, or connect to necklaces. If using fabric, use fabric glue to stick the shapes together with the thread in the middle.

MAKE A JEWELRY HOLDER

DID YOU DECORATE YOUR HANGERS?
With a wooden hanger and few eyehooks, you'll have the perfect place for your jewelry. You can even place rings over the center hook.

It can be frustrating digging around for that piece of jewelry that is perfect for your outfit. But once you have a slick jewelry holder, your worries of where to find that rad pair of earrings are over.

Jewelry Hanger

Use a piece of nature to hold your jewelry. Gather a clean branch with a decent amount of smaller branches on it. Tie a piece of ribbon or yarn from your kit to each end to hang necklaces, bracelets, earrings, and headbands.

Corkboard Jewelry Holder

A corkboard makes a great jewelry holder. Put thumbtacks on the board and hang your necklaces, rings, bracelets, and earrings from them. Use clear or colored thumbtacks depending on your taste.

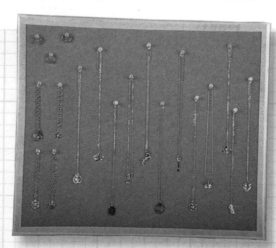

#instaTip:
This can also work as a cute gift box for a gift card or small trinkets for friends and family.

Mint Box Earring or Earbud Holder

1 Cover a tin with white acrylic paint for the base color.

2 Once the white paint dries, paint the color of your choice.

3 Put a bit of Mod Podge on the surface of the tin. Then add one of the patterned papers from the back of the book to the tin top.

4 Smooth the paper to remove any creases.

5 Cover the entire box and add a layer of Mod Podge over the paper so the pattern doesn't peel off.

Mod Podge is a type of glue that also protects decorated surfaces. If you don't have any Mod Podge, you can use white glue.

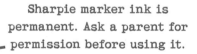
DECORATE YOUR KICKS

You know it's all about the shoes! So why not show your feet a little love with glitter, sequins, and words for your shoes?

WHAT YOU'LL NEED:

[ ] Glue

[ ] Gems, sequins, or studs

[ ] Sharpie markers

Sharpie marker ink is permanent. Ask a parent for permission before using it.

Glitz & Glam

Make the toes stand out with gems or sequins! Glue the gems or sequins with a dab of glue. If you get too much glue squishing out, use a toothpick to clean it from between the gems.

The studs come with prongs that you can push through the fabric of your shoe and bend down with pliers, so they stay in place.

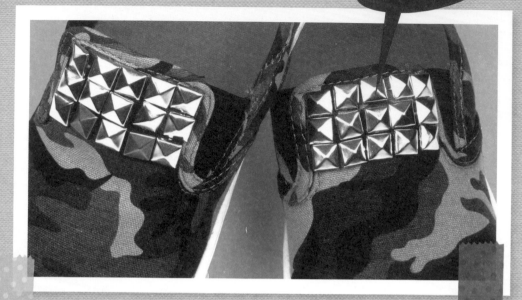

Stick on studs.

Put a word or image on each toe.

Glue on crystals.

#ShoeLove

BALLERINA
CONVERSE LACES

This can be done with any color Converse shoe.
Black looks the coolest and pink looks the cutest.

First let's look at how much ribbon you will need.

#instaTip: Remove the old laces from your shoes to use as a guide. Make the new ribbon laces twice as long as your old shoelaces.

1 Use a thick ribbon the color of your choice, though white is very ballet! Weave the laces through the holes. You may need to bend the ribbon in half to fit through the holes at first. Once they are through the holes, you can fluff.

2 Once you have completely laced the shoe, crisscross the ribbon above your ankle and around the lower part of your calf.

3 Wrap in crisscrosses a few more times if desired.

4 Make a knot on the inside of your leg. Roll the excess ribbon and tuck under the wide part. This may take a bit of practice, but once you get it down, you'll love this fresh spin on Converse shoes.

Lace or fabric Converse tongue

Cut lace so that it wraps around the top of the tongue. Use strong glue to stick each side to the tongue.

Use a Sharpie to color the lace holes and toes.

[WARNING] Ask the parentals if you can use Sharpie markers. These are permanent and can stain clothing, carpet, and upholstery.

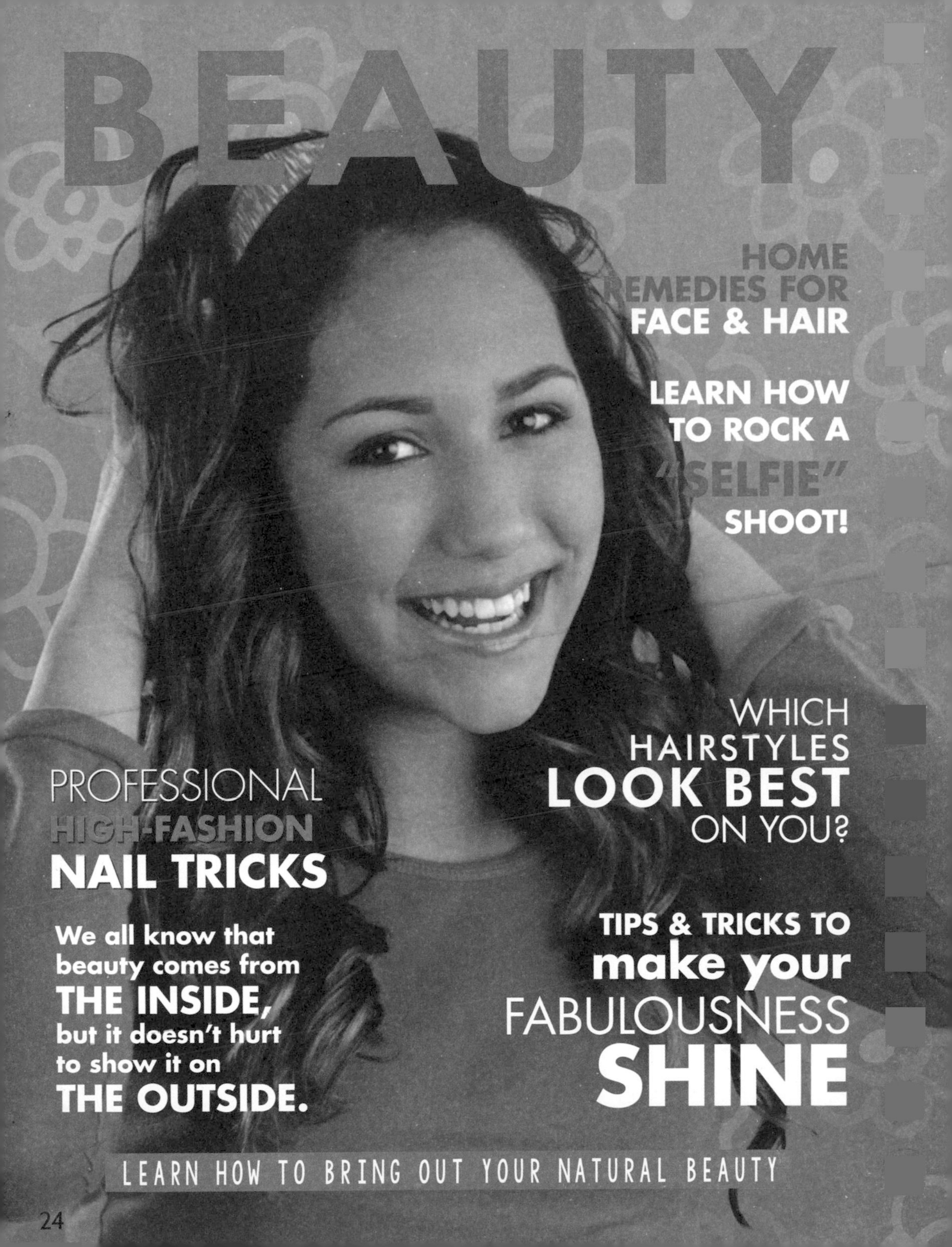
BEAUTY
HOME REMEDIES FOR FACE & HAIR
LEARN HOW TO ROCK A "SELFIE" SHOOT!
WHICH HAIRSTYLES LOOK BEST ON YOU?
PROFESSIONAL HIGH-FASHION NAIL TRICKS
We all know that beauty comes from THE INSIDE, but it doesn't hurt to show it on THE OUTSIDE.
TIPS & TRICKS TO make your FABULOUSNESS SHINE
LEARN HOW TO BRING OUT YOUR NATURAL BEAUTY

#hairandmakeup

#loveyourself

BEAUTY TIPS IN THIS SECTION:

Pages 26-27: Hairstyles That Look Good on You

28-29: DIY Hair #Obsessories

30-31: Fanatic Bun Addict

32: Nail Basics

33-35: Fancy Nail Art You Can DO

36-37: Natural Beauty Tips

38-39: Make Your Own Sugar Scrub

40-41: How to Take a Selfie That's an #InstaHit

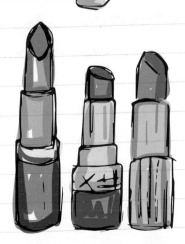

Write down some beauty tips you want to try

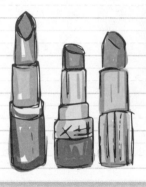

WHO INFLUENCES HOW YOU LOOK?

Check all that apply.

[ ] Me

[ ] My friends

[ ] Boys

[ ] My parents

[ ] Celebs

[ ] Singers

[ ] Models

[ ] Magazines

[ ] Social media

[ ] Paris

[ ] New York

[ ] London

[ ] L.A.

HAIRSTYLES
THAT LOOK GOOD ON YOU

What does your hair say about you?

Are you a hair fashionista or just going with the flow of your gorgeous locks? What looks best on you: short or long hair? Check out a few of these different styles to find out. Take a few selfies and determine what feels good to you and fits your personality the best! Share your hair selfies with your friends and see which styles they like best!

Messy or clean

Wavy or straight

Up or down

Short or long

Hair accessories are the perfect addition to your wardrobe. And they're easy to make, too!

Quick and Easy Brooch Headband

Use an elastic headband and connect a vintage or new brooch. Adjust the placement of the brooch when it's on your head.

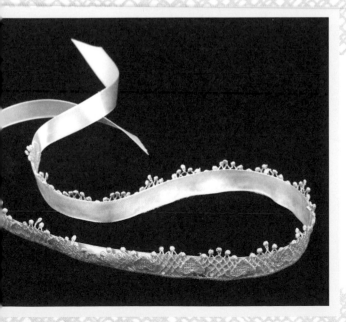

Lace & Ribbon Headband

Cut out a lace shape. Weave ribbon through the holes on one side of the lace to the other. When it's tied to your head, make sure the ribbon is on the bottom side of the lace, touching your head.

Hair Comb Happy

WHAT YOU'LL NEED:

[ ] A hair comb
[ ] 2 ft. (61 cm) of two
    different-colored yarns

WHAT TO DO:

1. Find two strips of different-colored fabric and a hair comb.

2. Tie a knot into the fabric at one end of the comb.

3. Weave one strand of fabric in and out of the comb one way.

4. Repeat with the second strand of fabric.

5. Then weave each fabric back individually.

6. Tie a knot and cut off any excess fabric.

Try other embellishments like jewels, old earring or necklace pieces, pearls, beads, or buttons.

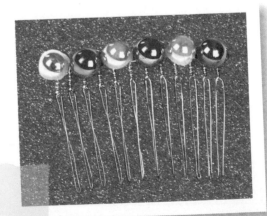

Beaded Hair Comb

Add beads to your hair comb with clear nail polish.

FANATIC BUN ADDICT

Time for a hair-venture!
Choose your own crazy and creative hair-venture
that works with your style!

Double Braid Bun

1 Put your hair in a high ponytail.

2 Separate your ponytail into two
sections.

3 Loosely braid each section and
secure each braid with a tiny
hair elastic.

4 Twist the braids around the
ponytail holder, pinning as you
go. Fluff and loosen parts to
provide a bit more volume.

To Die For!

#instaTip:
For a different look: Split the ponytail
with a top half and bottom half. Braid the top
half and wrap the single braid around the
ponytail holder and pin.

The Messiest of Messy Buns

1 Put your hair in a ponytail on top of your head. Optional: spray with a bit of hair spray.

2 Use a comb or brush to tease bottom of ponytail (closest to the hair tie).

3 Loosely wrap teased ponytail around ponytail band.

4 Secure with bobby pins. Tease and loosen as desired.

TO TEASE HAIR, TAKE A CHUNK OF HAIR AND HOLD AWAY FROM HEAD. With your other hand, take a comb and bring it to the tip of your hair. Move the comb from the tip to the base of your head. No need to be rough! Move the comb slowly at first to get a feel for the speed that helps create a bit of volume for your unique hair type.

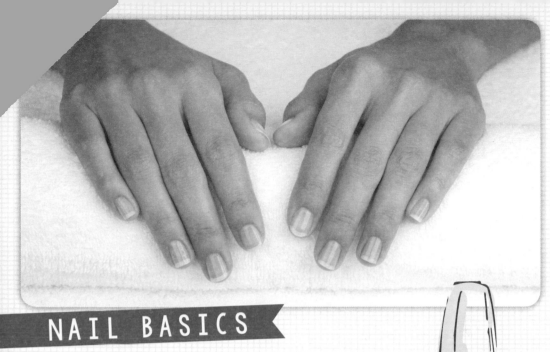

NAIL BASICS

To get nail crazy, you first need to NAIL down the basics. Here are a few nail-tastic tips to get you started.

1 Wash your hands before painting your nails.

2 Gently push back your cuticles.

3 Find a good primer. This will help color stick to your nail better and will also keep the color from soaking into your nail, which will make it easier to remove when you're ready to move on to the next color!

4 Pick the perfect color.

5 Find a good topcoat. This will keep your polish from chipping as well as give it extra shine!

6 Give your nails time to dry. If you need to speed things up, let your nails dry for two minutes. Then dip them into ice cold water for three minutes. Or use a hair dryer on COOL.

GREAT NAILS— AN INSIDE JOB

If you want strong, beautiful nails to paint, you'll need to eat right. Beautiful nails are an inside job. They especially love biotin, a B-vitamin. Talk to your parents about what you're eating.

FANCY NAIL ART YOU CAN DO

Ombre Nails

WHAT YOU'LL NEED:

[ ] Nail polish color of choice
[ ] White nail polish
[ ] Aluminum foil
[ ] Popsicle stick

WHAT TO DO:

1 Choose your nail polish color.

2 Paint your thumb the color straight out of the bottle.

3 Make four puddles of the nail polish color on aluminum foil.

4 Add a drop of white nail polish to the first puddle, two drops to the next, and so on.

5 Use a popsicle stick to mix the white in with the nail color. You'll notice the colors getting lighter with each puddle.

6 Apply to nails in color descending order from darkest (index finger) to lightest (pinkie).

These nails would be a great style to wear to the beach.

Sharpie Nail Art

Use a fine-tip Sharpie to add details to your painted nails. All Sharpie colors, including black and metallic, can give awesome effects. Be sure to apply over dry nail polish and apply a clear topcoat when you're done with the drawing.

#instaTip:
Make sure you have a covered work surface. Sharpies are permanent markers and can stain skin, clothes, carpet, and upholstery.

Sweet & Sparkly Nails

The next time you paint your nails try adding a bit of sparkle with sugar. First paint your nails the color of your choice. When the color coat is drying, sprinkle the sugar on top of each nail. Let your nails dry completely. Add a clear topcoat to secure the sugar. That's it! Super sweet and sparkly nails.

#OhSoSweet

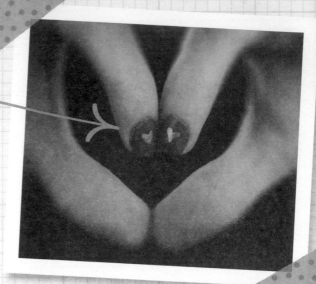

Washi Heart or Diamond Stencil

WHAT YOU'LL NEED:

[ ]   Red nail polish
      (or color of choice)

[ ]   Gold Sharpie
      (or color of choice)

[ ]   4 in. (10 cm) piece
      of washi tape

[ ]   Scissors

WHAT YOU DO:

1   Paint your nails with the base color and
    let dry completely.

2   Fold a piece of washi tape in half,
    sticky side together.

3   Cut half a diamond or half a heart into the
    middle of washi tape where it is creased.

4   Open the washi tape strip to view the full shape.

5   Place washi tape stencil over your nail.

6   Use the Sharpie to color over the stencil
    you made.

7   Let this dry completely, and gently pull off the
    washi tape stencil.

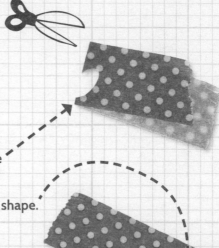

NATURAL BEAUTY TIPS

Keep yourself **looking and** feeling fresh, clean, and beautiful with these homemade natural beauty products and tips.

Looks gorgeous and tastes great! Win-win!

Gorgeous and vibrant lip color from powdered drink mix

WHAT YOU'LL NEED:

[ ] Fruity powdered drink mix packet

[ ] Small bowl

[ ] Q-tips

[ ] Petroleum jelly

WHAT YOU DO:

1 Grab your packet of fruity powder and pour it into a bowl.

2 Dampen your finger slightly and dip into powder mix.

3 Pat your lips with the powdered drink mix. Gently rub it onto your lips.

4 Use a dampened Q-tip to smooth out any bumps.

5 Add a bit of a petroleum jelly for shine.

For a lip gloss to take on-the-go, mix powder directly with petroleum jelly and keep in an airtight container.

#LipVictoryIsMine!

Make a Greek yogurt facemask

[ ] Headband

[ ] Hair tie (if you have long hair)

[ ] Cotton balls

[ ] Small container Greek yogurt

[ ] 1 tablespoon (15 ml) honey

Don't forget to take before, during, and after selfies!

Greek yogurt is a natural exfoliator, and honey helps moisturize your skin.

WHAT YOU DO:

1 Use a hair tie to pull back your hair and a headband to move the hair off of your face.

2 Mix the honey with the Greek yogurt.

3 In the bathroom, use a cotton ball to apply the yogurt mix to your face.

4 Leave the mixture on for ten minutes.

5 Rinse with lukewarm water.

Bonus: You can choose to rinse after the ten minutes, or add another layer of the yogurt mix and leave on for another five minutes.

#instaTip #1

Apply 3 tablespoons (45 ml) of honey and a cup of yogurt (any flavor!) to wet hair and let sit for three minutes. The honey will hydrate your hair, and the yogurt will give it shine.

#instaTip #2

Mix a little bit of baking soda with water and apply it to your face for a low-key cleanser.

Sugar scrubs not only smell and look fantastic, they exfoliate and moisturize your skin, too.

Make Your Own Snow Cone Sugar Scrub

WHAT YOU'LL NEED:

[ ] 1 cup (200 g) sugar

[ ] 3 bowls

[ ] 1 teaspoon (5 g) cherry powdered drink mix

[ ] 1 teaspoon (5 g) berry blue powdered drink mix

[ ] $\frac{1}{3}$ cup (90 ml) coconut oil

[ ] Clear cup

WHAT YOU DO:

1   Add $\frac{1}{3}$ cup (70 g) of sugar to each bowl.

2   Add 1 tsp. (5 g) of cherry powdered drink mix to one bowl.

3   Add 1 tsp. (5 g) berry blue powdered drink mix to another bowl.

4   Leave one bowl with just white sugar.

5   Add about 1 tablespoon (15 ml) of coconut or olive oil to each bowl.

6   Once combined, layer each sugar scrub on top of the other in a clear container. Sweet!

#SummerSkinDelight

#YUMMY!

These make great gifts for friends and family!

Orange Creamsicle Sugar Scrub

WHAT YOU'LL NEED:

[ ] 2 tsp. (10 g) orange zest (lemon or lime are great too!), or the juice of an orange

[ ] 1 cup (200 g) white sugar

[ ] 1 tsp. (5 ml) honey

[ ] ¼ cup (60 ml) olive oil

[ ] ½ tsp. (2.5 ml) vanilla extract

[ ] Small Mason jar

Try grape seed or almond oil instead of olive or coconut oil.

WHAT YOU DO:

#EasyPeasy! Mix all of the ingredients together and put them in the glass Mason jar.

Make or print out a cute label to put on the outside of the jar for an extra-special touch.

39

HOW TO TAKE A SELFIE
THAT'S AN #INSTAHIT!

You never know when an opportunity will come up to be on camera, whether it's a video shoot, a video chat, or the classic selfie. Always be selfie-ready by following these few #SelfieStardom tips.

1 Keep mascara and lip gloss on hand

2 For all of those perfect headshot selfies, stay relaxed by wearing comfy pants—no one is going to see them anyway! All you need is a stylish top. That's what you call a little bit of selfie magic. ;D

3 Keep binder clips handy for a quick DIY tripod. This might be a good time to pull out that washi tape and decorate your binder clips!

4 Use your earbuds' PLAY button to take pictures. This will help create some distance between you and your camera. Or use a selfie stick.

5 Find a spot with good natural light. If you're inside, stand close to a window. If you can't find a spot with natural light, find a spot with a lamp in front of you (not behind).

6 Take the selfie straight on or slightly above eye level. Having the camera slightly above highlights your cheekbones. #InstaGorgeous

7 Use a camera timer. This will give you time to check your angles and get to the spot you want. Wait to smile until the last second or two so that you don't have that strained smile look on your face.

8 When taking a full body/ outfit selfie, stand in front of a full-length mirror. Put your hand on your hip and cross your legs to look casual and cute.

MORE →

1

#cute

3

hello!

8

6

look **NOW**

Keep a scarf handy for those times you're lounging around the house in an old, grungy T-shirt. The scarf is a beloved go-to trend that will easily cover up and stylize any bad outfit for a headshot selfie.

THE DECOR

#RoomOfHerOwn

HOW TO
Make
Your
ROOM
PERFECT

GET
ORGANIZED!

HOW TO DECORATE
YOUR ROOM WITH
STYLE

D.I.Y.
room
DECOR
MADE EASY

#MYpersonalspace

#WhereIrock

TIPS FOR DECORATING YOUR ROOM

Pages 44-45 : How to Decorate Your Room with Style

46-47 : How to Organize Your Room

48-49 : Make Some Wall Art

50-51 : Phrase and Flower Bouquets

What are the **top 10 changes** you want to make to your room?

1
2
3
4
5
6
7
8
9
10

Where do you find inspiration?

Check all that apply.

[ ] My friends
[ ] Pics from web
[ ] Store sales
[ ] Magazines
[ ] Social media

[ ] TV
[ ] Paris
[ ] New York
[ ] London
[ ] L.A.

How to decorate your
ROOM WITH STYLE

Create a whole slew of cool, stylish, and creative environments in your room. This is your hibernation station, so we want it to be as true to your heart and style as possible.

Check out these awesome ideas and projects that will help you decorate and organize your room.

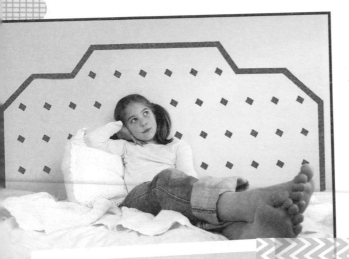

Make a washi tape headboard

IS YOUR BED ON THE FLOOR? NO PROBLEM. You can make a headboard out of washi tape. And it can be whatever style appeals to you!

Make washi tape frames for your photos and posters.

FRAMES CAN BE REALLY EXPENSIVE, especially when you want a lot of them. No problem. Make frames using washi tape. It's supersmart and stylish!

D.I.Y. poster board chalkboard

[ ] Black poster board

[ ] Washi tape

[ ] Removable poster tape

WHAT YOU DO:

1 Tape black poster board to the wall using removable poster tape.

2 Add a washi tape border around the poster board.

3 Only use real chalk (not chalk markers) if you plan on erasing your messages.

#InstaTip X: Cut the poster board into smaller pieces for multiple small chalkboards.

D.I.Y. dry erase board

FIND AN OLD PICTURE FRAME WITH THE GLASS AT A GARAGE SALE. It makes the perfect dry erase board. Paint the frame and add colorful paper or fabric behind the glass for a fun background.

#FrameWow

Pull yourself together, dude! Having a spot for everything is key. Even if you need a spot just for random things, at least you have a spot.

Shoebox organizer

A SHOEBOX IS THE PERFECT STORAGE BOX! Paint or cover the outside. Make a label so you know what goes in the box. Put these on a dresser, under your bed, on your desk, or in your closet. If you have different things you want to organize, glam it up a notch by adding toilet paper rolls or bottles to the bottom to create little compartments.

Mason jars, soda bottles, water bottles, and pickle or olive jars are perfect for this kind of decorating!

Old jar storage

RECYCLED JARS MAKE A GREAT PLACE TO HOLD SCHOOL SUPPLIES, ART SUPPLIES, OR EVEN JEWELRY, LIKE BRACELETS. Apply glue to the bottle. Then wrap the bottles or jars with yarn or cover with glitter. Make cute labels for each bottle.

MAKE SOME WALL ART

Take the dull and boring walls of your room and make them fab with some wall art! Spruce them up with photos, posters, record albums, or flags. Here are a few ideas to get you started.

Use your photos and posters to add pizzazz to your walls.

USE THE STICKERS THAT CAME WITH YOUR KIT to

create phrases on your selfies, friends, and school happenings. Cut out shapes from the patterned paper in the back of this book. Glue to parts of the picture. Glue on jewels and sequins, too. Or add some washi tape for a splash of color. Add as much as you want or keep it simple! Tape your decorated photos to the wall above your dresser, desk, or bed–wherever you like!

#GlamTwist:

For an extra pop of fun, create a frame for your wall art using a cereal box.

1 Cut out the front panel of the cereal or cracker box.

2 Tape your photo in the center of the panel.

3 Leave cereal box frame as is or cover it in fabric or the patterned paper to give it your personality.

4 Tape the cereal box frame to your wall.

More wall art ideas:

- ✳ British flag
- ✳ Giant tree
- ✳ Old record albums
- ✳ Starry night sky
- ✳ Dream catcher
- ✳ Old movie camera or photo camera

- ✳ Lion
- ✳ Mountain landscape
- ✳ Beach scene
- ✳ Anchor/wooden ship
- ✳ Bunch of balloons floating through space

Phrase & Flower Bouquets

WHAT YOU'LL NEED:

[ ] One of your decorated bottles or jars

[ ] Printed words

[ ] Straws or pencils

[ ] Tissue paper (favorite colors)

[ ] Glue

[ ] Scissors

[ ] Stapler

WHAT YOU DO:

To make the words:

1 Pick out your favorite words. Write each one on a piece of colorful paper or print them from the computer.

2 Cut out each word in a shape–heart, square, star, or circle. *Tip: If you decide on a square, make a border around the edges with washi tape for extra glam.*

3 Place the word shape facedown on a flat surface. *Tip: To find the center, make an "X" from corner to corner.*

4 Add a drop of glue to the center. Place the pencil eraser or straw in the center of the cutout. Press it down and hold until slightly dry.

To make the flowers:

1 Cut colorful tissue paper into 6-inch (15.2 cm) squares.

2 Layer tissue squares on top of one another.

3 Cut out a flower shape.

4 Staple the middle so all layers stay together.

5 Pull each layer upward one by one.

6 Use a pencil or straw as the stem just like you did the words. Put a little bit of glue in the center of the backside of the flower. Push the bottom layer of tissue down over the glue and hold in place. Let dry.

Fluff the flower petals, add the words, and you have a beautiful "floral" decoration for your room or maybe a gift for a friend.

#GlamTwist:

Try using photos instead of words for a fun twist!

PARTY FUN

Eeeeek
PARTY EXCITEMENT
OVERLOAD!

HOMEMADE
decorations
will rock the scene!

IMPRESS
your friends
with the
PERFECT PARTY

HOW TO
CELEBRATE
everything

52

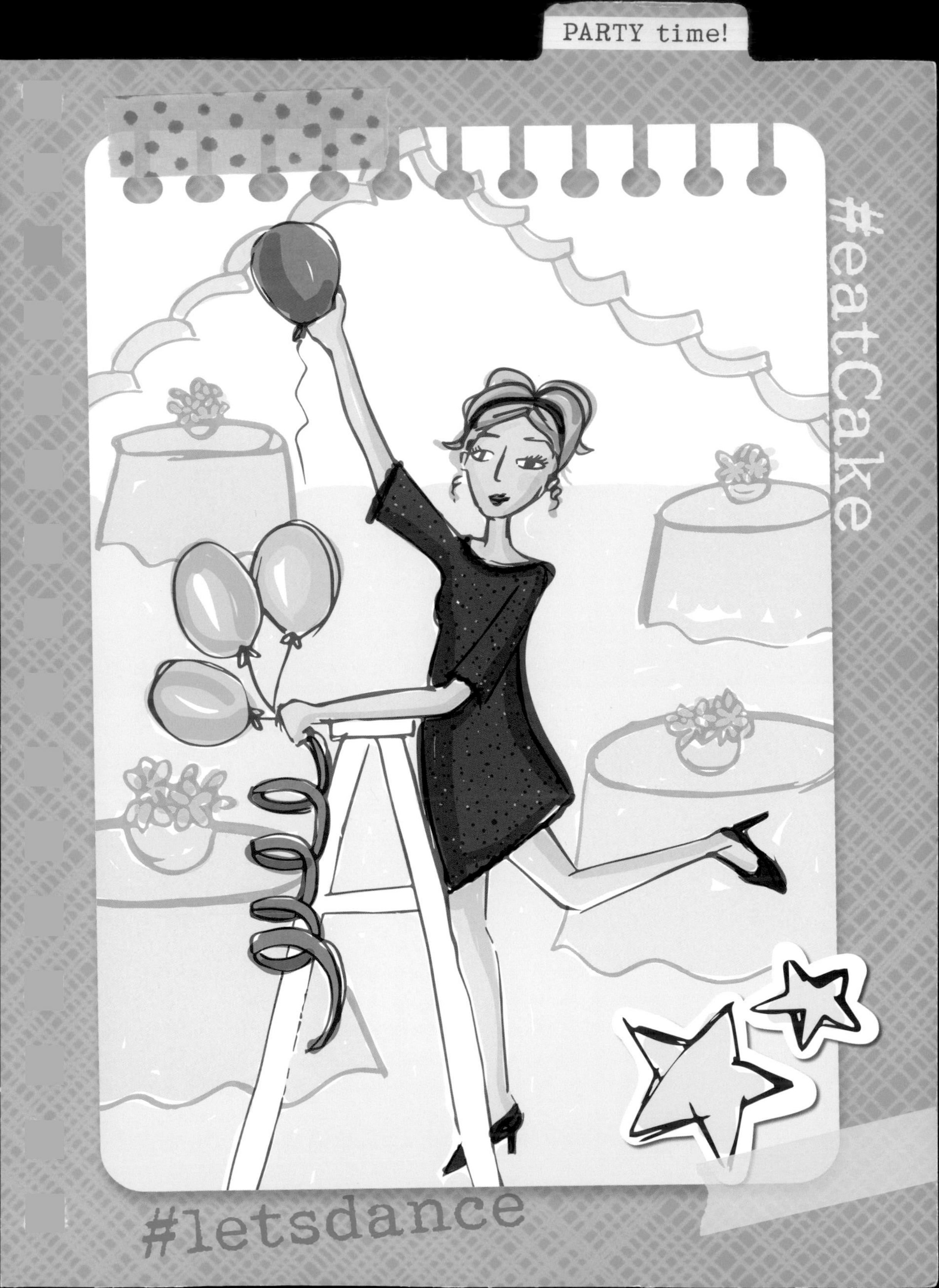
PARTY time!
#eatCake
#letsdance

TIPS FOR THROWING AN AWESOME PARTY

Pages 54-55: What kind of party?

56-57: Decorations – Make a party garland

58: Tulle and fabric balloons

59-61: Photo booth basics

62-63: Photo booth scavenger hunt

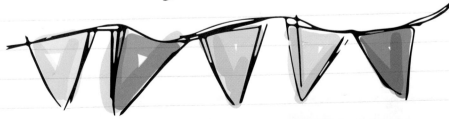

Let's get this
PARTY STARTED!

Let's get real, just about everything is worth celebrating. And who doesn't love a good party? This is your opportunity to hang with friends, have a great time, and impress them with your crafting and activity-planning skills. Make your party the most memorable of the year! In this section, learn how to plan the perfect party, from themes to favors to decorations, and much more!

PARTY ESSENTIALS TO REMEMBER WHILE PLANNING:

1. Theme
2. Location
3. Invitations
4. Decorations
5. Games and activities
6. Food (arguably the most important part!)
7. Favor (a cute trinket for everyone to take home)

Figuring out a theme is the best place to start. Once you figure out the theme, you'll know what kind of location will hold it best, what kind of decorations to make, what kind of activities to plan, and what kind of food to devour!

THINK ABOUT WHAT YOU ARE CELEBRATING.
Is it a holiday? Is it a birthday? Is it the end of the school year? Whatever you are focusing on, make sure the theme runs throughout everything you do to make it memorable. Here are some theme ideas and color palette examples to help get you started.

What's your party idea?
Write it down here.

P.S. Try to think of two to three colors to focus on for your theme. That way decorations won't get too crazy and clash.

Beach, Pool, or Summer Party
✓ Pink, orange, and yellow

Under the Sea
Blue, green, and coral

Fiesta
Green, pink, blue, and orange

Spa party
✓ Teal and pink

Hollywood
✓ Gold, black, and red

Sleepover
Different shades of purple

Valentine's Party
Red, pink, and white

DECORATIONS
Make some fun garlands

Garlands are a fun and easy decoration for any party. Tape any image you desire to string to fit your theme of choice. Follow the directions below to make a summer-themed garland.

WHAT YOU'LL NEED:

[ ] Tape
[ ] String or ribbon
[ ] Popsicle stencil
[ ] Patterned paper
[ ] Wooden popsicle sticks
[ ] Scissors

Look for the popsicle stencil that came with your kit.

WHAT YOU DO:

1 Using the Popsicle stencil, cut out popsicle shapes from the colored paper in the back of the book or choose your own paper. Tape a popsicle stick to the bottom as shown in the picture.

2 Place the popsicles upside-down in a line.

3 Lay string or ribbon on top of the popsicles so they are in the middle or slightly toward the top.

4 Place a piece of tape over the string so it is connected to the back.

5 Hang from window, stair banister, door, or any wall.

More themed garland ideas!

BEACH PARTY: beach ball and sunglasses ✓

FIESTA: sombrero, piñata, maracas

HOLLYWOOD: glittery stars, microphone, camera ✓

SPA: lipstick and nail polish ✓

VALENTINE'S DAY: Candy or glittery hearts, lips, cupid ✓

FOR ANY PARTY: print pictures of you and your friends. Cut images into fun shapes.

#BringTheBling

#GlamTwist: Use the star and heart stencils in your kit to make a glamorous garland.

#instaTips!

- If you have cookie cutters in your kitchen, these make great stencils to trace shapes for garland. #EasyPeasy

- Any garland (or decoration for that matter) can be used as a decoration for your room when the party is over!

- Create one kind of garland or three different garlands and layer them.

- Use cupcake liners to create a pretty garland. Any color or patterned cupcake liner will do. Tape the backs to ribbons as you would a cut out shape.

- Create a garland with cereal or candy! Pick a cereal or candy that is shaped like an "O," and place them on a ribbon, yarn, or string.

#InstaFloatWOW

Tulle or Fabric Balloons

Balloons are a great way to add beauty to your party. And when they're covered with tulle or fabric you have floating style.

WHAT YOU'LL NEED:

[ ] Any color, helium-filled balloon

[ ] 1 yd. (1 m) Fabric pattern of choice or tulle (cut into square)

[ ] Ribbon

[ ] Scissors

What else can you decorate with these beautiful balloons?

WHAT YOU DO:

1 Blow up balloons and tie the end.

2 Take the fabric or tulle square, and place the top of the balloon in the center of the fabric square.

3 Bring all four corners to the tip of the balloon and cinch together around tied spout.

4 Use pretty ribbon to tie the cloth around the bottom.

5 Tie individual balloons to different locations around the party room—tie to chairs, tie in bunches, let them sit on the floor, or use helium to help them float.

#instaTip: To make a balloon garland, make sure each balloon has a little bit of extra ribbon tied to the cinched area. Using a long piece of ribbon, tie them to the ribbon, keeping one balloon 6 inches (15.2 cm) from the next.

Photobooth Basics

Photo booths are a great way to add fun and a lot of laughs to your party!

Find a good spot with natural light — preferably close to a window (not right in front of it).

PHOTO BOOTH BACKGROUND

★ Make a cute backdrop by gluing colorful pom-poms to a white sheet.

★ Find a colorful blanket.

★ Decorate area with themed garlands.

★ Use wrapping paper, colorful cellophane, aluminum foil, streamers, ribbon, ripped fabric, or newspaper.

★ A blank wall will do just fine, too.

A giant frame makes an extra-chic prop (no glass or backing needed)!

Photo booth props

Find props around the house: sunglasses, ties, hats, jewelry, scarves, or make your own.

WHAT YOU'LL NEED:

[ ] $\frac{1}{4}$ inch (6.4 mm) Wooden dowels

[ ] Construction paper, stiff felt, or computer printouts

[ ] Stencil (that comes with your kit)

[ ] Scissors

[ ] Tape

WHAT YOU DO:

1 Use the stencil to trace an image or print out an image from the computer.

2 Cut out your images of choice.

3 Turn the picture facedown. Place the wooden dowel on the side. This way it won't block your face when you hold it up.

4 Place tape over the wooden dowel so there is enough on both sides to stick to the paper and hold the dowel in place.

#instaTip: Text your friends a picture of them from the photo booth so they'll remember the fun!

RANDOM PROP IDEAS: tiara, mustache, beard, maracas, cowboy hat, birthday hat, foam finger, lollipop, lips, or bow.

What can you come up with?

Photo booth

WHO SAID YOU HAVE TO STAY IN ONE SPOT TO TAKE PART IN A PHOTO BOOTH? This is a fun twist on a photo booth. Why not make a game out of it?

#SoPhotoSilly

How you play:

1) Pair up with a partner to form a team. You can have as many teams as you want (if you have a lot of people at your party, make teams of three or four).

2) Give each team a list of items that they need to have on them to take the selfie. For instance, if you have five props to find — sunglasses, lips, wacky bag, hat, or sombrero — each team will try to find these items and take a photo with them and get back before the other teams.

3) Each team is given a list of clues as to where the props are hidden throughout the house and yard. (Even if your friends don't know the house and yard very well, you can give them a quick tour of the layout. Be sure to let everyone know which areas are off limits.)

4) The first team to take a picture with all of the props, wins!

At the end of the game, put all pictures up on a screen, whether TV or computer, and have fun going through all of the crazy and wacky pictures!

COOKING

#InstaChef!

Dig into some
"NOM-NOM"
RECIPES

LET'S GET
cookin'!

PUTS ON
**OVEN
MITTS**
& LICKS LIPS

#mixitup

YUMMY THINGS TO MAKE AND SHARE

Pages 66-69: Kitchen Basics & Safety

70: Sweet Treats!

71: Fairy Bread

72-73: Cereal Bars

74-77: Popsicles

78: Frozen Banana Treats

79: S'more Pops

80-81: After-school snacks

82-83: Homemade Granola Bars

84-85: Sweet Popcorn, and then some!

86: Party Drinks

87: Chocolate-covered Peanut Butter Pretzels

88-89: Simple Cupcake & Cupcake Fondue

90-93: That's a Wrap!

94-96: Waffle Sandwiches and Pizzas

My Insanely Delicious Recipes!

Cooking and baking is an art form. Think of the kitchen as your palette and the ingredients as your paints! Whether it's healthy, delicious, sweet, or savory, it's all here!

TAKE PICTURES OF YOUR FOOD ALONG THE WAY!

This will help you keep track of what you've made. Plus, it's always fun to share a delicious recipe with a friend. Remember what we said about finding natural light for your selfie? Well, the same goes for food! And be careful. Don't get a shadow of your hand in the picture! Move around a bit until you find the right angle to take the shot.

Kitchen
BASICS & SAFETY

Your experience will be a lot more fun if you learn some kitchen basics! It's time to take a quick look at some basic kitchen tools, staying safe in the kitchen, and how you can make easy dishes and recipes that taste great!

Baking and Cooking Basics

💜 Baking can be very precise. Try to follow the recipes as closely as you can for the best results!

💜 The classic baking temperature is 350°F (180°C), but check the recipe. The temperature will vary for different food items.

💜 Remember to grease your pans before adding dough or batter (unless a recipe specifically says not to). Nothing is worse than a delicious treat ruined because it sticks to the pan!

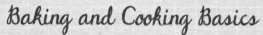

#BakingBummer!

♥ Don't open the oven in the middle of baking. It lets in cooler air, which will lower your baking temperature. If you want to check on your food, use the oven light.

♥ When you think a cake might be done, open the oven and insert a toothpick in the middle. If it comes out clean, it's done! If it comes out a little gooey, keep in the oven for a few more minutes.

♥ If a package or recipe says it will be done in a certain amount of time, check a few minutes early just to make sure it's not done early. Ovens and stoves vary in temperature and baking times. Burnt cookies are sad!

#BakingBummer!

♥ Put a lid on a pot of water to help it boil faster!

♥ When working with dough, add a little flour to your work surface so the dough doesn't stick to the counter or your hands!

Safety Tips

💜 Start by asking your parents to help you with baking and using the stove. Always, always get their permission.

💜 Ovens can get very HOT! Make sure to ALWAYS have an adult help you use the oven and stove.

💜 Always, always, always remember to turn the oven or the stove top off when you're done.

💜 Sometimes the pot's or pan's handle can get hot. Use an oven mitt to avoid burns.

💜 When it's time to take food out of the oven or off the stove, have a pad or trivet ready to set the pan on so you don't burn the counter.

💜 Wash your hands before you start prepping and cooking, and throughout to keep germs away from food and to keep the different types of food from spreading germs to each other.

♥ Use one cutting board for meat and another cutting board for vegetables. Wash your knife, prepping tools, and hands in between prepping these items to avoid moving germs from one to the other.

♥ There are a lot of sharp tools in the kitchen. Be extra safe by asking an adult to help you use knives.

♥ If you are not using a certain tool, put it away or put it in the kitchen sink away from your work area.

♥ Keep your counters as clean as possible.

♥ Clean up when you're done prepping.

Microwave Tips

♥ Some of these recipes suggest using the microwave. It's a great option for melting chocolates or other ingredients.

♥ Food, bowls, and plates can still get really hot, so always use oven mitts or a towel when taking a dish out of the microwave.

SWEET TREATS!

ADMIT IT. YOU HAVE A SWEET TOOTH, RIGHT? You lay in bed at night dreaming of dancing cupcakes and ginormous chocolate fountains. This is your chance to wake up and smell the yummy! Indulge in these sweet recipes as a delicious reward after a healthy meal.

Answer the questions to discover your favorite treat!

WHAT KIND OF SWEETS DO YOU LIKE?

a. Frozen: Popsicles, ice cream.
b. Baked: Cakes, cupcakes, cookies, brownies, pies
c. Candy, candy, candy

WHAT ARE YOUR FAVORITE COMBOS?

a. Peanut butter and chocolate
b. Chocolate hazelnut spread and banana
c. Cookies and milk

WHAT DO YOU TOP YOUR SWEET TREAT WITH?

a. Sprinkles — sugar, shapes, jimmies, circles/dots
b. Crushed cookies
c. Cereal
d. Nuts
e. Chopped candy bars
f. Caramel, chocolate, and peanut butter sauce
g. Marshmallows and marshmallow fluff

Write your answers here.

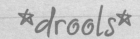

BRING A LITTLE MAGIC TO YOUR MORNING WITH A PRETTY PLATE OF FAIRY BREAD! This toast will brighten your morning with a punch of color. Use as a surprise sleepover snack or a bright breakfast party treat. If only everything could have sprinkles on it!

WHAT YOU DO:

1 Toast white bread.

2 Slather on the butter or cream cheese!

3 Add sprinkles.

4 Use a cookie cutter to cut into fun shapes.

Fairy Bread

[ ] White bread

[ ] Rainbow sprinkles

[ ] Butter or plain cream cheese (try strawberry or blueberry cream cheese for an extra pop of flavor)

Try a chocolate hazelnut spread instead of cream cheese!

Try this!
Don't use the cookie cutter. Cut the crust off and roll the bread like a wrap.

#delish

71

Cereal bars

[ ] 3 tablespoons (47 g) butter

[ ] 1 bag marshmallows

[ ] 2 drops food coloring (optional)

[ ] 6 cups (150 g) crispy rice cereal

[ ] Wooden spoon

[ ] Large saucepan

[ ] 8 in. x 8 in. (20 cm x 20 cm) glass or tin square pan

[ ] Oil spray or more butter to grease the pan

TAKE A STROLL DOWN THE CEREAL AISLE OF YOUR LOCAL GROCERY STORE, or use whatever you have in the kitchen cabinet! Almost all cereals can be turned into a scrumptious, crispy treat. Let's do a basic crispy rice cereal bar first.

WHAT YOU DO:

1 Put stove burner on LOW. Add butter to melt.

2 Stir the marshmallows until they have melted.

3 If using food coloring, add the color to the melted marshmallow mixture and stir until blended.

4 Take the saucepan off of the stove and add the rice cereal to the hot marshmallow mixture.

5 Grease the 8 in. x 8 in. (20 cm x 20 cm) pan.

6 Pour the rice mixture into the pan.

Warning! Get an adult to help you with the stove.

Remember, #SafetyChef

Twist it up! Cereal Pops

FOLLOW THESE DIRECTIONS TO MAKE SOME FUN AND FANCY CEREAL POPS

1 Once the cereal has cooled, cut the treats into shapes using cookie cutters.

2 Add sticks or straws to the center of the cute cereal pops.

Try dipping these yummy treats in melted chocolate or add a topping, like sprinkles, nuts, crushed cookies, or dried fruit.

#instaTip: Add a few drops of food coloring to the melted marshmallow to match a party color scheme or to add a sense of whimsy to this delectable treat.

Popsicles

POPSICLES ARE A REFRESHING SUMMER SNACK that can be a healthy treat, too. Mix and match flavors. Choose a base, and then choose a mix to add. It's that easy.

#EasyPeasy

Write down some popsicles you'd like to create in the space below.

TURN UP THE BASE!

- Pudding – any flavor you like, but some of the most popular are chocolate, vanilla, butterscotch, and strawberry.

- Jell-O – yes, Jell-O! Not only does Jell-O sell a multitude of flavors but the gelatin will keep your Popsicle from dripping too much as you eat it.

- Juice – grape, orange, cranberry, apple, pomegranate, or what's your favorite?

- Soda

- Yogurt

- Flavor packets and water – lemonade, fruit punch

- Juice box

- Smoothies

Mix it up!

WHAT ELSE WILL YOU PUT IN YOUR POPSICLE?

- chocolate candies
- gummy candies
- sprinkles
- granola, cereal
- nuts
- peanut butter
- honey
- chopped fruit
- crushed Pop-Tarts
- crushed cookies
- crushed cereal

MAKE YOUR POPSICLE DREAMS COME TRUE!

Dream up your ultimate popsicle concoctions here.

Popsicle molds are sold at many department and grocery stores, but if you don't happen to have one, no worries! Use an ice cube tray, a cupcake tin, or small plastic cups to make mini popsicles. Fill the molds with your popsicle mixtures of choice. Then cover the cup or ice tray with a layer of aluminum foil. Poke a popsicle stick or tooth pick through aluminum foil into the popsicle mixture. The aluminum foil will help keep the stick in place while the popsicle freezes. Let them freeze overnight.

Yummy Candy Popsicles

[ ] Gummies

[ ] Lemon-lime soda

[ ] Popsicle mold

**These yummy popsicles
are perfect for cooling
off on a hot summer day!**

#sugarRUSH

If you don't want this
popsicle to be overly
sweet, replace some or all
of the lemon-lime soda with
plain soda water.

WHAT YOU DO:

1 Choose your gummies: worms, bears,
O's, fish, or fruit snacks.

2 Add ¼ cup (50 g) to each popsicle mold.

3 Pour lemon-lime soda into the popsicle
mold to the fill point.

4 Place in freezer for at least 2 hours
or overnight.

5 When you're ready to eat one, let the
popsicle sit on the counter for a few minutes
to loosen the popsicle from the mold.

#SuperCool

fun

> **FINALLY!** We've figured out how to enjoy a cinnamon roll in the hot summer sun!

WHAT YOU DO:

1 Beat cream cheese until it is smooth.

2 Mix in the vanilla pudding powder and cinnamon. Beat until completely combined with cream cheese.

3 Add milk to mixture.

4 Pour into the mold and place in the freezer for at least 2 hours or overnight.

Cinnamon Roll Pop

[ ] 1 box of instant vanilla pudding mix

[ ] 4 ounces (125 g) of softened cream cheese

[ ] 3 cups (750 ml) milk or vanilla almond milk

[ ] 1 tablespoon (6 g) cinnamon

[ ] Hand mixer

[ ] Large bowl

[ ] Popsicle mold

Note: If using regular milk, add ½ teaspoon vanilla extract.

To easily release the popsicles, place mold in a bit of warm water for 15 seconds.

Frozen Banana Treats

Peel and cut a banana in half. Place a popsicle stick into the bottom of the banana half. Ask a parent to help you melt white, milk, or dark chocolate in the microwave. Dip the banana half in the chocolate. Roll it in nuts, cookie pieces, candy, or sprinkles. Place the banana treats on a cookie sheet lined with waxed paper. Place the entire sheet in the freezer and let freeze overnight. #SuperYum

#instaTip: Put the popsicle stick in the banana BEFORE freezing!

#TotallyFruity

#JustLikeCamping

S'more Pops

[ ] Graham cracker cookies

[ ] Large marshmallows

[ ] $\frac{1}{4}$ cup (45 g) chocolate chips

[ ] Microwave-safe bowl

Warning! Get an adult to help you with the microwave! The chocolate can get super hot.

WHAT YOU DO:

1 Put two marshmallows on a stick.

2 Put the chocolate chips in the bowl and melt them in the microwave.

3 Dip both sides of the marshmallows in melted chocolate.

4 Stick a piece of graham cracker on either side. Place on tray, and then in the fridge for 10 minutes until the chocolate hardens.

Pounding the books all day is tough work.
Does your brain need a pick-me-up? Eat these snacks
when you get home or bring them to school to eat
right before an extracurricular activity.

#BrainFood

Fruit Skewers

Mix and match your favorite fruits or
use one of the suggestions below!

Slice ingredients
and layer one after
the other

Rainbow Blast

Strawberries, cantelopes,
green grapes, blueberries,
red grapes

Tropical Breeze

Pineapples, strawberries,
red grapes, kiwis

Fruity Fall

Bananas, peaches, grapes,
pineapples, oranges,
blueberries

#instaTip: Squeezing a bit of lemon
juice on sliced apples will keep them
from turning brown!

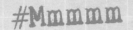

Frozen Yogurt Fruit Skewers

Add blueberries to the skewer. Roll the skewer in vanilla or blueberry yogurt and place in freezer.

Strawberry Shortcake

On a skewer, layer strawberries, pound cake cut with a small round cookie cutter, and marshmallow or whipped topping.

#LayeredNom

Fruiternutter

On a skewer, layer a crustless PB & J sandwich cut into fours, with banana or strawberries.

#instaTip: If you have to stay after school, make these the Sunday before the school week starts so you can save time in the morning. Pack them with an ice pack to keep them cool.

#Granola

TRY THIS RECIPE FIRST.
Then experiment with mixing up a few different ingredients to make a scrumptious and personalized granola bar.

No need to bake!

Make granola bites by using a mini cupcake tin, an ice cube tray, or simply by cutting into smaller pieces.

Granola bars

[ ] 2 cups (170 g) oats

[ ] ½ cup (13 g) crispy cereal such as a crispy rice cereal

[ ] ¾ cup (135 g) dried cranberries

[ ] ¼ cup (45 g) white chocolate chips

[ ] ¼ cup (60 g) melted butter

[ ] ¼ cup (50 g) brown sugar

[ ] ¼ cup (60 mL) honey

[ ] ½ teaspoon salt (2.5 g)

[ ] 1 teaspoon (5 mL) vanilla extract

[ ] 1 teaspoon (2 g) cinnamon

[ ] Large bowl

[ ] Saucepan

[ ] Wooden spoon

[ ] 8 in. x 8 in. (20 cm x 20 cm) glass or tin pan

[ ] Cooking spray

Warning! Get an adult to help you with the stove!

WHAT YOU DO:

1 In a bowl, stir together oats, crispy rice, cranberries, and white chocolate chips.

2 Add the melted butter, brown sugar, honey, and salt to the pan over medium heat. Stir to combine.

   Note: Add ¼ cup (57 g) peanut butter to sugar/honey mixture for a nuttier flavor.

3 Cover and heat for 2 minutes.

4 Take the mixture off the heat, and add the cinnamon and vanilla.

5 Combine the wet ingredients with dry.

6 Press down into greased pan.

7 Place in fridge for 20 minutes to cool. Slice into bars.

Try a few of these ingredients in your next batch:

NUTS – peanuts, almonds, cashews, pistachios

SEEDS – pumpkin, sunflower

DRIED FRUIT – cranberries, blueberries, raisins

MILK/DARK/WHITE CHOCOLATE CHIPS – even butterscotch or caramel

SPRINKLES

SHREDDED COCONUT

YOGURT DRIZZLE

THIS IS THE PERFECT TREAT FOR PARTIES, sleepovers, holidays, and of course, a light, but sweet afternoon snack.

Bubblegum popcorn

[ ] 1 Bag of microwave popcorn

[ ] ½ cup (90 g) white chocolate chips

[ ] Red food coloring

[ ] ½ teaspoon (2.5 ml) raspberry extract

[ ] Large saucepan

Warning!
Help needed from an adult!

WHAT YOU DO:

1 Pop the popcorn.

2 Get an adult to help you melt the white chocolate in the microwave or over low heat on the stove.
Note: If microwaving, remember the bowl will be hot when it's time to take it out. Have a pair of oven mitts handy!

3 Add a drop of red food coloring (don't add too much or the white chocolate will turn red instead of pink!).

4 Then add ½ teaspoon (2.5 ml) of raspberry extract.
Note: If you don't have raspberry extract on hand, don't sweat it! This popcorn is just as delicious without it.

#instaTip: Extracts add an extra pop of flavor. Try vanilla, almond, orange, lemon, or even coffee extract next time!

Cupcake Popcorn

Cupcake popcorn is a great birthday or slumber party treat! You'll need the same ingredients as the Bubblegum Popcorn, but switch the raspberry extract for vanilla. Be sure to add some sprinkles!

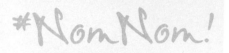

WHAT YOU DO:

1 Pop the popcorn and melt white chocolate. No need to add food coloring this time.

2 Add a ½ teaspoon (2.5 ml) of vanilla extract to the melted white chocolate.

3 Drizzle the white chocolate mixture over the popcorn and add sprinkles.

4 Place a spoonful into a cupcake liner.

French Toast Popcorn

For a fun weekend afternoon treat, melt 2 tablespoons (32 g) of butter and stir in ½ teaspoon (1 g) of cinnamon. Drizzle over popped popcorn. Then, add 1 tablespoon (15 ml) of maple syrup to the white chocolate and melt together. Drizzle that over popcorn, too.

Surprise Party Drink

Add cotton candy to ginger ale and the fun begins. The cotton candy turns into tiny balls that float along with the fizz.

Lime Fizz

Pour lemon-lime soda into a glass. Add about 4 drops of green food colors (or the color of your choice). Stir it up so the drink looks green. Then, a slice of lime, and you have a Fizzy Lime Drink.

Chocolate-Covered Peanut Butter Pretzels

[ ] 1 cup (266 g) creamy peanut butter

[ ] 2 tablespoons (32 g) softened butter

[ ] ½ cup (75 g) powdered sugar

[ ] ¾ cup (150 g) brown sugar

[ ] 1 Bag pretzels

[ ] 1 Bag milk chocolate chips

[ ] Rainbow sprinkles

[ ] Parchment paper

[ ] Baking tray

[ ] Microwave-safe bowl

Try dark or white chocolate for a yummy twist!

WHAT YOU DO:

1 Line a baking tray with parchment paper.

2 Mix peanut butter and butter together. Add powdered and brown sugar. Once completely mixed, roll peanut butter into small balls.

3 Place a peanut butter ball between two pretzels. Smoosh a bit and place on a tray or cookie sheet lined with wax paper. Put the tray in the freezer.

4 While the pretzels are in the freezer, melt the chocolate in a microwave-safe bowl for 1 minute.

5 Check the chocolate every 20 seconds and stir. The stirring will help the chocolate melt.

6 Take the tray of pretzel yummies out of the freezer and dip the pretzels in the melted chocolate.

7 Add sprinkles. Stick back in freezer for at least 10 minutes so the chocolate hardens.

It doesn't take much to melt chocolate. When heating in the microwave, check every 20 seconds and stir to make sure the chocolate doesn't burn. Stirring will help the chocolate melt, too.

Simple cupcakes

[ ] 2 cups (300 g) flour

[ ] $\frac{1}{2}$ teaspoon (1 g) salt

[ ] 2 teaspoons (4 g) baking powder

[ ] $\frac{1}{2}$ cup (125 g) butter, softened

[ ] 1 cup (200 g) sugar

[ ] 2 eggs

[ ] 1 cup (250 ml) milk

[ ] 1 teaspoon (5 mL) vanilla extract

[ ] 2 bowls

[ ] Wooden spoon

[ ] Cooking spray or cupcake liners

[ ] Cupcake tin

[ ] Hand mixer

WHAT YOU DO:

1 Preheat oven to 350°F (180°C).

2 Mix together the butter and sugar.

3 Add eggs one at a time. Fully mix before adding the next egg.

4 Stir in the vanilla.

5 In a separate bowl, stir together all dry ingredients (flour, salt, baking powder).

6 Add the dry ingredient mix to the butter mixture.

7 Stir in the milk until completely combined.

8 Pour batter into a greased and lined cupcake tin.

9 Place in the preheated oven and bake for 18-24 minutes.

Don't forget to take a selfie while you're making these treats!

Quick frosting

You'll need ½ cup (125 g) unsalted, softened butter, 2 cups (300 g) powdered sugar, and 1½ (7.5 ml) teaspoons vanilla extract. First, cream ½ cup (125 g) of unsalted, softened butter until fluffy. Gradually add 2 cups (300 g) powdered sugar and mix as you add. When the sugar is completely mixed in, add 1½ teaspoons (7.5ml) of vanilla extract. Then, pour in 2 tablespoons (30 ml) of milk and mix until combined. Add a few drops of food coloring to make different colors.

Cupcake fondue

Use simple cupcake recipe from previous page, but use a mini cupcake tin to make mini cupcakes. To make frosting glaze, mix 3 cups (450 g) of powdered sugar with 2 tablespoons (30 ml) of corn syrup and ⅓ cup (75 ml) juice, milk, or water.

Pour frosting glaze into a medium-sized bowl. Put different-colored sprinkles, sugars, and other toppings in smaller bowls. If you don't have fondue sticks, use pretty straws, forks, or skewers. Place the mini cupcakes on the stick. Dip into glaze. Sprinkle with topping.

When you make the frosting glaze, try orange juice or pink lemonade for yummy flavor and a fun pop of color.

Use water or milk if you just want to add other toppings like sprinkles.

#SprinkleFun!

THAT'S A WRAP!

There is a whole world of sandwiches and wraps to explore. Here are a few variations, perfect for when you're chompin' at the bit for an insanely good meal but don't have a lot of time. Don't be afraid to try your own mixing and matching.

#NoSandwichFear

Peanut Butter Breakfast Wrap

[ ] Flour or wheat tortilla.

[ ] 2 Tablespoons (32 g) peanut butter

[ ] A drizzle of honey

[ ] $\frac{1}{4}$ cup (21 g) granola

[ ] Sliced strawberries

[ ] Sliced bananas

Try this wrap with cashew butter, almond butter, sunflower butter, or chocolate hazelnut spread. Yum!

WHAT YOU DO:

1 Spread peanut butter to cover tortilla.

2 Top with strawberries, bananas, and granola.

3 Drizzle honey over the toppings and roll it up.

Strawberry Wrap

Slather strawberry cream cheese on tortilla wrap. Layer sliced strawberries over cream cheese. Roll and cut 2 inch (5 cm) pieces. Perfect for a light snack or summer sandwich! For a bit of crunch, add sliced almonds.

#instaTip: For a sweeter treat, add a drizzle of honey.

#TotallyFruity

91

Turkey Wrap

Spread garden vegetable cream cheese over a whole-wheat tortilla. Add layers of turkey, carrots, and lettuce. Roll it up and slice it on a diagonal.

#instaTip: Use hummus instead of cream cheese. Or try adding a few snap peas!

Apple Wrap

Spread cream cheese on one side of whole-wheat tortilla. Ask an adult to help you slice some apples really thin. Any kind of apple works. Add a layer of the thinly sliced apples. Drizzle honey over the apples. Roll up the tortilla. Eat up!

Warning! Get an adult to help you with the skillet part!

Kick it up a notch by grilling the sandwich over medium heat. Butter the pan. Heat until both sides are golden brown.

For a healthy
twist, use a piece
of romaine lettuce
to wrap contents
instead of a flour
tortilla.

Thai Peanut Wrap

The peanut butter sauce
[ ] ⅓ cup (76 g) peanut butter
[ ] ⅓ cup (90 ml) honey
[ ] ¼ cup (60 ml) soy sauce
[ ] ¼ cup (60 ml) water

Other ingredients
[ ] Wheat tortilla
[ ] Broccoli slaw or lettuce
[ ] Shredded carrots
[ ] Roasted peanuts
[ ] Grilled chicken strips

Optional: Cucumber slices and bean sprouts

Add a dash
of red pepper
flakes, if you
like it spicy!

WHAT YOU DO:

1 Lay flour tortilla flat.

2 Add broccoli slaw,
shredded carrots,
roasted peanuts,
grilled chicken strips,
and drizzle with
peanut butter sauce.

3 Fold up two
opposite sides of
the tortilla over the
filling and roll up
the tortilla.

4 Cut each wrap in half.
Serve with remaining
peanut sauce.

#VEGdelish

Note: If you are a vegetarian,
try this wrap without the chicl

Waffle sandwiches? Yes, waffle sandwiches!

There is no such thing as a boring sandwich when there is a waffle involved. Use any brand of frozen waffle. Shoot for a whole-wheat waffle to pack in extra good stuff.

#instaTip: There are a ton of different waffle sandwiches that you can make with stuff in your kitchen. Try a PB&J waffle sandwich, or maybe a vegetarian. There is no end to this waffle madness!

1 Slather mustard onto one waffle.

2 Add the ham and cheese.

3 Then top with another frozen waffle.

4 Heat skillet on medium. Add a little butter to pan.

5 Place the sandwich in the prepared pan.

6 Cook on the first side for 3 to 4 minutes.

7 Then flip to the other side and press down on the cooked side with spatula. Cook this side for another 3 to 4 minutes, or until the cheese is melted and both sides are golden brown.

Ham & Cheese Waffle Sandwich

[ ] Ham

[ ] Cheese (Swiss, American, or Cheddar are great choices)

[ ] Mustard or mayo (optional)

[ ] 2 frozen waffles

[ ] Butter knife

[ ] Spatula

[ ] Skillet

[ ] 1 teaspoon butter

Warning! Get an adult to help you with the skillet part!

Waffle Breakfast Sandwich

Put a breakfast spin on the waffle sandwich by putting scrambled eggs, sausage, bacon or Canadian bacon, and American or Cheddar cheese between the waffles. It makes a yummy way to start the day.

Waffle Pizza

Toast a frozen waffle. Add marinara or pasta sauce to fill crevices to the edge. Top with mozzarella cheese and pepperoni (or other toppings of your choice). Place in microwave until cheese melts, about 45 seconds, or put in the oven at 450°F (230°C) for 8-10 minutes (until cheese bubbles).

#instaTip: Toasting in the oven will give you a crispier waffle.

#ToppingsGalore

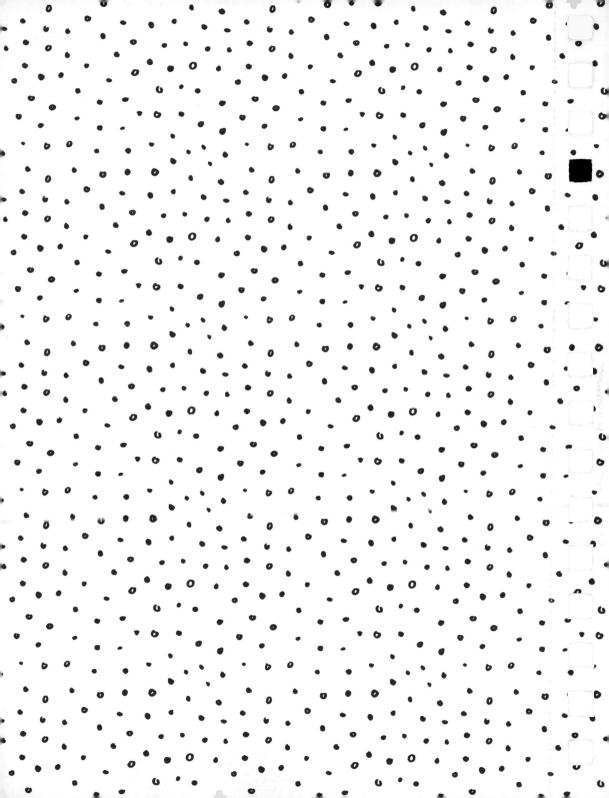